White-Collar Crime in the Shadow Economy

Petter Gottschalk • Lars Gunnesdal

White-Collar Crime in the Shadow Economy

Lack of Detection, Investigation and Conviction
Compared to Social Security Fraud

Petter Gottschalk
BI Norwegian Business School
Oslo, Norway

Lars Gunnesdal
Manifest Analysis
Oslo, Norway

Open access for this book was sponsored by BI Norwegian Business School

ISBN 978-3-319-75291-4   ISBN 978-3-319-75292-1   (eBook)
https://doi.org/10.1007/978-3-319-75292-1

Library of Congress Control Number: 2018937892

© The Editor(s) (if applicable) and The Author(s) 2018. This book is an open access publication (corrected publication June 2018).
Open Access This book is licensed under the terms of the Creative Commons Attribution 4.0 International License (http://creativecommons.org/licenses/by/4.0/), which permits use, sharing, adaptation, distribution and reproduction in any medium or format, as long as you give appropriate credit to the original author(s) and the source, provide a link to the Creative Commons license and indicate if changes were made.
The images or other third party material in this book are included in the book's Creative Commons license, unless indicated otherwise in a credit line to the material. If material is not included in the book's Creative Commons license and your intended use is not permitted by statutory regulation or exceeds the permitted use, you will need to obtain permission directly from the copyright holder.
The use of general descriptive names, registered names, trademarks, service marks, etc. in this publication does not imply, even in the absence of a specific statement, that such names are exempt from the relevant protective laws and regulations and therefore free for general use.
The publisher, the authors and the editors are safe to assume that the advice and information in this book are believed to be true and accurate at the date of publication. Neither the publisher nor the authors or the editors give a warranty, express or implied, with respect to the material contained herein or for any errors or omissions that may have been made. The publisher remains neutral with regard to jurisdictional claims in published maps and institutional affiliations.

Cover pattern © Melisa Hasan

Printed on acid-free paper

This Palgrave Pivot imprint is published by Springer Nature
The registered company is Springer International Publishing AG
The registered company address is: Gewerbestrasse 11, 6330 Cham, Switzerland

The original version of this book was revised. An erratum to this book can be found at https://doi.org/10.1007/978-3-319-75292-1_11

Contents

1 White-Collar Crime Research 1

2 Theory of Crime Convenience 15

3 Tip of the Crime Iceberg 27

4 Expert Elicitation for Estimation 37

5 Research Challenges 49

6 More Research Results 57

7 Student Elicitation for Estimation 67

8 Social Security Fraud 73

9 Other Macroeconomic Estimations 89

10	**White-Collar Crime Detection**	111
Erratum to: White-Collar Crime in the Shadow Economy		E1
Conclusion		135
References		139
Index		153

List of Figures

Fig. 4.1 Fraction of white-collar criminals that are brought to justice 40
Fig. 4.2 Estimation of white-collar crime based on seven approaches 45
Fig. 4.3 Tip of the iceberg for white-collar crime 46
Fig. 8.1 Estimation of the magnitude of different forms of financial crime 76

LIST OF TABLES

Table 3.1	White-collar crime experts on the elicitation research panel	33
Table 4.1	Estimation based on levels of white-collar criminals	41
Table 4.2	Estimation based on categories of white-collar crime	42
Table 4.3	Estimation based on categories of white-collar crime victims	43
Table 4.4	Estimation based on gender of white-collar criminals	44
Table 4.5	Estimation based on seven approaches	45
Table 4.6	Lower and upper bounds for the estimate of white-collar crime	46
Table 6.1	Seven different expert estimations of the magnitude of white-collar crime	60
Table 7.1	Estimation based on levels of white-collar criminals	68
Table 7.2	Estimation based on categories of white-collar crime	69
Table 7.3	Estimation based on categories of white-collar crime victims	69
Table 7.4	Estimation based on gender of white-collar criminals	70
Table 7.5	Student's estimation based on five approaches	71
Table 7.6	Distribution of iceberg elements for white-collar crime	72
Table 8.1	Comparison of estimates for white-collar crime and social security fraud	80
Table 9.1	Shadow economy as a fraction (%) of GNP (Schneider et al. 2010)	93
Table 10.1	Detection of white-collar crime	115
Table 10.2	Comparison of journalist and non-journalist detected white-collar criminals	116
Table 10.3	Financial crime categories by detection sources	117
Table 10.4	Characteristics of stimulus in detection of white-collar crime	127

Introduction

Abstract Our starting point is our database of those who annually are convicted of white-collar crime in Norway. Convicts commit financial crime amounting to 1 billion Norwegian Kroner (NOK) annually—the tip of the iceberg. Our calculations suggest that the iceberg may be more than ten times bigger than what is visible. White-collar crime competes with other kinds of financial crime for police resources. For example, white-collar crime competes with social security fraud for financial crime investigations, the latter receiving a lot more public scrutiny. We make a comparison with previous estimates of social security fraud in Norway. While social security fraud is estimated to cause economic damage totaling 10 billion NOK annually, white-collar crime probably causes total damage of 12 billion NOK.

Keywords Convenience theory • Crime detection • Database • Estimation • Expert elicitation • Norway • Social conflict theory • Social security fraud • Tip of the iceberg • White-collar crime

The tip of the iceberg is a small, noticeable part of a problem, the total size of which is really much greater. The tip of the iceberg is only the beginning and just a small indication of a larger problem, one that is much bigger than it seems. The tip of the iceberg is a metaphor: Floating icebergs have a significant proportion of their mass below the surface of the water. We believe this is also the case for white-collar crime. The tip of the iceberg is the few offenders who are caught, prosecuted, and convicted. The iceberg itself includes the many offenders who are never brought to justice.

This book describes research where we attempt to estimate the iceberg size. We examine, through expert elicitation, what experts who have uncovered some forms of white-collar crime, as well as students, think and believe about the magnitude, causes of, and reactions to, this phenomenon.

The starting point for our research is a known number, namely our database of those who are convicted of white-collar crime annually. Convicts commit financial crime to the tune of well over 1 billion Norwegian Kroner (NOK) ($125,000) annually. One billion is like scratching the surfacing or observing the tip of the iceberg.

Our calculations do indeed suggest that the iceberg may be more than ten times bigger than what is visible in Norwegian courts. When only one out of 12 billion NOK is visible, it may mean that only about one in ten white-collar offenders is sentenced, and that more than 90 percent of the iceberg is below the surface of the symbolic water.

This research is important, as white-collar crime competes with other financial crimes for police resources. For example, white-collar crime competes with social security fraud in financial crime investigations, the latter receiving a lot more public scrutiny. We therefore introduce a comparison with previous estimates of social security fraud in Norway, which have also been attained through expert elicitation.

Such a comparison is highly relevant, since both social security fraud and white-collar crime represent serious forms of financial crime causing harm to both organizations and victims in society. While social security fraud is committed by people who basically need financial help from the community to live decent lives, white-collar crime is committed by individuals in the upper-echelons of society who abuse their positions to enrich themselves or organizations they are associated with. Since the two types of cases, in many ways, are two extremes of the spectrum of economic criminals, where one group mainly consists of losers and the other group mainly consists of winners in society, this book explores law enforcement against these two groups by applying social conflict theory. According to social conflict theory, the elite in society have developed laws and regulations that are often not intended for themselves.

The police have limited resources to investigate economic crime and have to prioritize their resources by dropping a large portion of cases

(Brooks and Button 2011). The question we ask here is: Should law enforcement primarily dismiss social security fraud cases or white-collar crime cases?

To enable prioritizing between social security fraud versus white-collar crime, criteria have to be applied. Criteria such as social concerns, political positions, ethical dilemmas, and other issues are certainly relevant. The consequences of prioritization can be found at the individual, organizational as well as national levels. In this book, we start by applying an economic criterion: What causes the largest financial loss; social security fraud or white-collar crime?

While social security fraud undermines our trust-based welfare system, it may be that white-collar crime undermines our entire trust-based social system. If the elite in society are abusing their positions for personal or organizational enrichment beyond legal boundaries, then it can create mistrust in most senior managers, whether they are in business, government or politics.

In this book, we show that while social security fraud in 2015 was estimated to cause economic damage totaling 10 billion NOK annually, white-collar crime is probably causing a total annual damage of 12 billion NOK.

This result may come as a surprise to the general public in Norway. When the leading Norwegian financial newspaper, *Dagens Næringsliv*, published an article some years ago about how law enforcement officials in Norway believe that only one out of four white-collar criminals is caught and brought to justice, the reaction was that this is unacceptable. Now, some years later, our experts believe that only one out of ten white-collar criminals are caught and brought to justice. Although there is some variation in procedure results, the average of 12 billion NOK seems to be a significant empirical result given a variety of approaches and a diverse group of experts.

All such estimates are subject to considerable uncertainty, and both calculations can be challenged and criticized. Subject to this uncertainty, we believe our estimate of 12 billion NOK for white-collar crime is better founded than the estimate of 10 billion NOK for social security fraud. One message from our research is that white-collar crime is just as serious—or even more serious—than social security fraud, and thus should be taken more seriously by police authorities to ensure equality before the law.

The final Chap. 10 in this book is concerned with white-collar crime detection by discussing crime signal detection.

The core of this book is concerned with the tip of the iceberg of white-collar crime (Chap. 3), the expert elicitation for estimating the magnitude of white-collar crime (Chap. 4), research challenges in estimating the unknown (Chap. 5), more research results from the expert elicitation (Chap. 6), student elicitation for estimating the magnitude of white-collar crime (Chap. 7), a comparison between the magnitude of white-collar crime and the magnitude of social security fraud (Chap. 8), and other estimations of the shadow economy in general (Chap. 9).

Chapter 1 introduces white-collar crime research, while Chap. 2 introduces the theory of convenience as an integrated explanation of the white-collar crime phenomenon. For readers who would like to learn more about white-collar crime research and the theory of convenience, we recommend other books by one of the authors: Gottschalk (2015, 2016, 2017a, b, c, 2018a, b, c).

References

Brooks, G., & Button, M. (2011). The Police and Fraud Investigation and the Case for a Nationalized Solution in the United Kingdom. *The Police Journal, 84*, 305–319.

Gottschalk, P. (2015). *Fraud Examiners in White-Collar Crime Investigations*. Boca Raton: CRC Press, Taylor & Francis Publishing.

Gottschalk, P. (2016). *Explaining White-Collar Crime: The Concept of Convenience in Financial Crime Investigations*. London: Palgrave Pivot, Palgrave Macmillan, Springer Publishing.

Gottschalk, P. (2017a). *Understanding White-Collar Crime: A Convenience Perspective*. Boca Raton: CRC Press, Taylor and Francis Publishing.

Gottschalk, P. (2017b). *CEOs and White-Collar Crime: A Convenience Perspective*. London: Palgrave Pivot, Palgrave Macmillan, Springer Publishing.

Gottschalk, P. (2017c). *Organizational Opportunity and Deviant Behavior: Convenience in White-Collar Crime*. Cheltenham: Edward Elgar Publishing.

Gottschalk, P. (2018a). *Investigating White-Collar Crime: Evaluation of Fraud Examinations*. New York: Springer Publishing.

Gottschalk, P. (2018b). *Fraud Investigation: Case Studies of Crime Signal Detection*. London: Routledge Publishing.

Gottschalk, P. (2018c). *Whistleblowing: White-Collar Fraud Signal Detection*. Cambridge: Cambridge Scholars Publishing.

CHAPTER 1

White-Collar Crime Research

Abstract One of the theoretical challenges facing scholars is to develop an accepted definition of white-collar crime. The main characteristic is that it is economic crime committed by a person of respectability and high social status in the course of an occupation. While Edwin Sutherland's concept of white-collar crime has enlightened sociologists, criminologists, and management researchers, the concept may have confused attorneys, judges and lawmakers. One reason for this confusion is that white-collar crime in Sutherland's research is both a crime committed by a specific type of person, and it is a specific type of crime. Later research has indicated, as applied in this book, that white-collar crime is no specific type of crime, it is only a crime committed by a specific type of person.

Keywords Convenience theory • Criminology • Definition • Edwin Sutherland • Gender perspectives • Occupational crime • Offence characteristics • Offender characteristics • Special sensitivity hypothesis • Social status

Ever since Sutherland (1939) coined the term "white-collar crime", there has been extensive research and debate on what to include and what to exclude from this offense category (e.g., Piquero and Benson 2004; Pontell et al. 2014; Stadler et al. 2013). In accordance with Sutherland's original work, convenience theory emphasizes the position and trust enjoyed by the offender in an occupational setting (Shapiro 1987). Therefore, the organizational dimension is the core of convenience theory where the offender has access to resources to commit and conceal financial crime.

The typical profile of a white-collar criminal includes the following attributes (Piquero and Benson 2004; Pontell et al. 2014; Stadler et al. 2013):

- The person has high social status and considerable influence, enjoying respect and trust, and belongs to the elite in society.
- The elite have generally more knowledge, money and prestige, and occupy higher positions than other individuals in the population occupy.
- Privileges and authority held by the elite are often not visible or transparent, but known to everybody.
- Elite members are active in business, public administration, politics, congregations, and many other sectors in society.
- The elite is a minority that behaves as an authority towards others in the majority.
- The person is often wealthy and does not really need the proceeds of crime to live a good life.
- The person is typically well educated and connects to important networks of partners and friends.
- The person exploits his or her position to commit financial crime.
- The person does not look at himself or herself as a criminal, but rather as a community builder who applies personal rules for his or her own behavior.
- The person may be in a position that makes the police reluctant to initiate a crime investigation.
- The person has access to resources that enable involvement of top defense attorneys, and can behave in court in a manner that creates sympathy among the public, partly because the defendant belongs to the upper class, often a similar class to that of the judge, the prosecutor, and the attorney.

However, one of the theoretical challenges facing scholars in this growing field of research is to develop an accepted definition of white-collar crime. While the main characteristic is the foundation—economic crime committed by a person of respectability and high social status in the course of an occupation—other aspects lack precision (Kang and Thosuwanchot 2017).

Edwin Sutherland

Edwin Sutherland is one of the most cited criminologists in the history of the criminology research field. Sutherland's work has inspired and motivated a large number of scholars in the field associated with his work. His ideas influence, challenge, and incentivize researchers. Sutherland's research on white-collar crime is based on his own differential association theory. This learning theory of deviance focuses on how individuals learn to become criminals. Differential association theory assumes that criminal behavior is learned in interaction with other persons.

Sutherland's (1939, 1949) concept of white-collar crime has been so influential for various reasons. First, there is Sutherland's engagement with criminology's neglect of the kinds of crime of the powerful and influential members of the elite in society. Next, is the extent of damage caused by white-collar crime. Sutherland emphasized the disproportionate extent of harm caused by the crime of the wealthy in comparison to the much researched and popular focus on crime by the poor, and the equally disproportionate level of social control responses. Third, there is the focus on organizational offenders, where crime occurs in the course of their occupations. A white-collar criminal is a person who, through the course of his or her occupation, utilizes respectability and high social status to perpetrate an offense. Fourth, the construction of the corporation as an offender indicates that organizations can also be held accountable for misconduct and crime. Finally, there is the ability to theorize the deviant behaviors of elite members. Many researchers have been inspired by Sutherland's groundbreaking challenge that mainstream criminology neglects the crime of the upper class and has a dominating focus on the crime of the poor. This was a major insight that began a dramatic shift and broadening in the subject matter of criminology that continues today.

Sutherland's long-lasting influence on criminological, sociological and, more recently, on management thinking is observable across the globe, but in particular in the United States and Europe. Sutherland exposed crime by people who were thought of as almost superior, and who apparently did not need to offend as a means of survival. Businesspeople and professionals frequently commit serious wrongdoing and harm with little fear of facing criminal justice scrutiny. It is often the case that poverty and powerlessness is the cause of one kind of crime while excessive power can be the cause of another kind of crime.

Sutherland exemplified the corporation as an offender in the case of war crime where corporations profit heavily by abusing the state of national emergency during times of war. Corporate form and characteristics as a profit-maximizing entity shape war profiteering. This is organizational crime by powerful organizations that may commit environmental crime, war profiteering, state-corporate crime, and human rights violations.

While Sutherland's concept of white-collar crime has enlightened sociologists, criminologists, and management researchers, the concept may have confused attorneys, judges, and lawmakers. In most jurisdictions, there is no offense labeled white-collar crime. There are offenses such as corruption, embezzlement, tax evasion, fraud, and insider trading, but no white-collar crime offense. Sutherland's contribution to the challenge of concepts such as law and crime can be considered one of the strengths of his work as he showed that laws and legal distinctions are politically and socially produced in very specific ways. For lawmakers, there is nothing intrinsic to the character of white-collar offenses that makes them somehow different from other types of offenses.

One reason for this confusion is that white-collar crime in Sutherland's research is both a crime committed by a specific type of person and a specific type of crime. Later research has indicated, as applied in this book, that white-collar crime is no specific type of crime; it is only a crime committed by a specific type of person. However, white-collar crime may indeed, sometime in the future, emerge as a kind of crime suitable for law enforcement as Sutherland envisaged it in his offender-based approach to crime, focusing on characteristics of the individual offender to determine the categorization of the type of crime.

Sutherland's broader engagement with criminological and sociological theory in general, such as his theory of differential association and social learning, has been and still is influential. One aspect of the theory of differential association—social disorganization—has had a significant influence on later researchers.

It must be noted that Sutherland's key constructs and definitions have divided criminology. Nelken (2012) suggests there is ambiguity about the nature of white-collar compared to ordinary crime. Croall (1989: 157) phrased the question "Who is the white-collar criminal?":

> White-collar crime is traditionally associated with high status and respectable offenders: the 'crimes of the powerful' and corporate crime. However, examination of one group of white-collar offences reveals that offenders were typically small businesses, employees, and those more properly

described as 'criminal businesses'. While this could be attributed to the 'immunity' of the corporate offender from prosecution, it can be argued that such patterns of offending reflect not only enforcement policies but also wider structural and market factors. Thus, analyses of economic and white-collar crime may concentrate overmuch on the corporate offender, and make over simplistic distinctions between 'corporate' and other varieties of white-collar offending.

Levi (2002) emphasized a wide socio-economic spectrum of fraud offending when discussing shaming and incapacitating business fraudsters.

OFFENSE CHARACTERISTICS

White-collar crime is illegal acts that violate responsibility or public trust for personal or organizational gain. It is one or a series of acts committed by non-physical means and by concealment to obtain money or property, or to obtain business or personal advantage (Leasure and Zhang 2017).

White-collar crime is a unique area of criminology due to its atypical association with societal influence compared to other types of criminal offenses. White-collar crime is defined in its relationship to status, opportunity, and access. This is the offender-based perspective. In contrast, offense-based approaches to white-collar crime emphasize the actions and nature of the illegal act as the defining agent. In their comparison of the two approaches, Benson and Simpson (2015) discuss how offender-based definitions emphasize societal characteristics such as high social status, power, and respectability of the actor. Because status is not included in the definition of offense-based approaches and status is free to vary independently from the definition in most legislation, an offense-based approach allows measures of status to become external explanatory variables.

Benson and Simpson (2015) approach white-collar crime utilizing the opportunity perspective. They stress the idea that individuals with more opportunities to offend, with access to resources to offend, and that hold organizational positions of power are more likely to commit white-collar crime. Opportunities for crime are shaped and distributed according to the nature of economic and productive activities of various business and government sectors within society.

Benson and Simpson (2015) do not limit their opportunity perspective to activities in organizations. However, they emphasize that opportunities are normally greater in an organizational context. Convenience theory, however, assumes that crime committed in an organizational context be called white-collar crime. This is in line with Sutherland's (1939, 1949) original work, where he emphasized profession and position as key characteristics of offenders.

White-collar crime research is a growing field with a number of scholars. Green (2007) discussed lying, cheating, and stealing, while Naylor (2003) developed a general theory of profit-driven crime. Some of the accumulated research will be presented in the theory of convenience. Crime-as-choice theory, as suggested by Shover et al. (2012) for white-collar crime, has links to convenience theory.

Offender Characteristics

The white-collar offender is a person of respectability and high social status who commits financial crime in the course of his or her occupation (Leasure and Zhang 2017). In the offender-based perspective, white-collar criminals tend to possess many characteristics that are consistent with expectations of high status in society. White-collar offenders display both attained status and ascribed status. Attained status refers to status that is accrued over time and with some degree of effort, such as education and income. Ascribed status refers to status that does not require any specific action or merit, but rather is based on more physically observable characteristics, such as race, age, and gender.

The main offender characteristics remain privilege and upper class. Early perception studies suggest that the public think that white-collar crime is not as serious as other forms of crime. Most people think that street criminals should receive harsher punishments. One explanation for this view is self-interest (Dearden 2017: 311):

> Closely tied to rational choice, self-interest suggests that people have views that selfishly affect themselves. Significant scholarly research has been devoted to self-interest-based views. In laboratory conditions, people often favor redistribution taxes when they would benefit from such a tax. This self-interest extends into non-experimental settings as well. For example, smokers often view increasing smoking taxes less favorably than non-smokers do.

In this line of thinking, people may be more concerned about burglary and physical violence that may hurt them. They may be less concerned about white-collar crime that does not affect them directly. Maybe those who are financially concerned about their own economic well-being will be more concerned about white-collar crime (Dearden 2017).

White-collar perpetrators have social power associated with different occupational activities across the society. Power and authority in the hands of individuals enable white-collar crime, with power essentially deriving from the positions individuals legitimately occupy.

Gender Perspectives

Research has suggested a relationship between gender and tax compliance, with men being more likely to commit tax offenses than women. Research on tax evasion has both an offender-based perspective and an offense-based perspective. Wealthy individuals have more opportunities to avoid tax compliance and to benefit more from it. In addition, circumventing tax compliance can be organized in a professional setting, where the business enterprise manipulates accounting for the purpose of tax evasion. Status affects the ability of individuals successfully to avoid detection or sanctions for non-compliance, and the opportunity to commit a variety of tax offenses is status based. Tax compliance can be the result of interaction between authority and expectations, where both authority and expectations are based on individual status.

The offense-based approach to defining white-collar crime is also fitting when examining tax offenses. The actions of being non-compliant dictate that the offense itself is considered a crime.

A special kind of tax offense is bank deposits in tax havens. As documented by Andersen et al. (2017: 2), banks help politicians and others transform petroleum rents and other assets into hidden wealth using bank deposits in tax havens:

> Political elites abuse public office to extract rents. Even moderate levels of political rents may have socially undesirable effects, through the adverse selection of political candidates and by distorting political incentives. In countries without strong democratic governance, political rents can be substantial and the economic and political consequences severe.

When white-collar offenders are brought to justice, Supernor (2017: 148) found that "a lot more women were given community service than men" because "women are considered homemakers for families, and the court systems do not want to punish a woman in a way that would take her away from her family".

Occupational and Business Crime

A distinction in white-collar offenses can be made between occupational crime and business crime. Occupational crime is committed by persons in an organizational setting for purely personal gain and to the detriment of the organization. Business crime is committed by or on behalf of the organization for profit or enhancement (Kang and Thosuwanchot 2017). Of course, in business crime organizations cannot commit illegal acts independently of human agents.

Occupational crime is typically committed under conditions of low levels of socialization and weak accountability. Employees may be unfamiliar with organizational goals or simply ignore organizational goals, while at the same time exerting efforts toward personal goals due to weak restraints by the accountability system. The presence of occupational crime may be symptomatic of larger failures in an organization's system since an organization without committed and accountable employees suggests a higher likelihood of failing in the end. Occupational crime tends to be committed by privileged individuals who feel no attachment to the organization, and who do so purely for personal gain (Kang and Thosuwanchot 2017).

Business crime, on the other hand, is typically committed under conditions of high levels of socialization and strong accountability. Employees not only identify with the organization but also its goals. The pursuit of organizational goals over individual goals does not imply the absence of crime. Rather, achievement of organizational goals becomes so important that if it cannot be done in legal ways, dedicated employees do it in illegal ways (Kang and Thosuwanchot 2017).

Both occupational and business crime is committed within the organizational context. Corporate crime is committed for business advantage and examples include cartels and corruption. Illegal price fixing and market sharing occur in cartels to enable participants in cartels to achieve more profits. Bribes are offered to potential customers, allies, and public officials to enable contracts and licenses (Leasure and Zhang 2017).

Convicted White-Collar Criminals

It is often argued that convicted white-collar criminals have a hard time in prison. They have to leave all their privileges and opportunities behind to join a community dominated by street crime inmates. This argument is formulated using the special sensitivity hypothesis, which suggests a relatively tougher everyday life for white-collar crime inmates compared to street crime inmates. However, empirical studies of white-collar inmates do not support the special sensitivity hypothesis. Rather, empirical studies support the special resilience hypothesis, which suggests that white-collar offenders are able to adapt to prison life more successfully than other inmates. In this section, we argue that the theory of convenience can provide support for the special resilience hypothesis.

If a white-collar criminal should end up in jail, defense attorneys work hard to make prison life as easy as possible for the client. Attorneys argue that it is much worse for a member of the elite to end up in prison than for other people. After a short while, the white-collar offender typically gets most of his freedom back in an imprisonment setting to avoid too much damage. However, research indicates that it is easier for a white-collar criminal than for a street criminal to spend time in prison. White-collar offenders tend to find new friends more conveniently, and they are able to sleep all night, while most other inmates may have trouble sleeping and making friends in prison (Dhami 2007; Stadler et al. 2013).

Evidence of neutralization by denial of responsibility can be found in autobiographies by white-collar criminals such as Bogen (2008), Eriksen (2010), Fosse and Magnusson (2004), and Kerik (2005). Bernard B. Kerik was the former New York police commissioner who served three years in prison. He seems to deny responsibility, to condemn his condemners, and to suggest normality of action. Evidence of neutralization can also be found in autobiographies by those who were accused of misconduct, but never prosecuted or convicted. An example is ex-Lehmann Chief Financial Officer Erin Callan who presents herself as a victim rather than an offender (Montella 2016).

In this chapter, we argue that there is lack of evidence for the special sensitivity hypothesis for white-collar inmates. The autobiography by Kerik (2005) is used in our case study of lack of evidence. Rather, there is support for the special resilience hypothesis that we discuss in terms of convenience theory in the next chapter.

Special Sensitivity Hypothesis

The idea that white-collar criminals are especially sensitive to imprisonment is based on the premise that they are of higher status than street criminals. They belong to the elite in society, and their fall from grace is much greater, since the higher people fly, the further they fall. White-collar offenders have a greater investment in the prevailing social order and have more to lose. Some argue that a belief is commonly held by those in the criminal justice system that white-collar offenders are ill equipped to adjust to the rigors of prison life. According to the special sensitivity hypothesis, the claim is made that white-collar offenders experience the pains of imprisonment to a greater degree than traditional street offenders.

Upon incarceration, they lose their direct influence and authority over people in business and private life, they lose their direct access to resources that enable them to do almost whatever they like, and they lose their self-identity characterized by position, trust, and profession. They enter a world that is foreign to them. They leave a hierarchy in society where they held positions at the top, and join a hierarchy in prison where they are far away from the top. Those with physical prowess and criminal connections, such as members of global biker gangs, rule prison life. White-collar offenders discover that they find few of their equals, similar to those they have socialized with for most of their lives. The majority in most prisons is populated by poor and minority group members. In North European prisons, for example, the majority consists of refugees and immigrants who ended up on the wrong side of the law.

The special sensitivity of white-collar offenders has been cited as a reason for the supposed leniency with which they have been punished traditionally. The argument is based on a study by Mann et al. (1979), who found that American judges handed down lighter sentences to white-collar criminals because of an *a priori* assumption that they would not cope well in the prison environment. Judges apparently assumed that white-collar offenders were not socialized into the ways of the majority of the prison population, simply because they come from the upper echelon of society. Therefore, it was assumed that the experience from arrest to imprisonment would be especially traumatic for white-collar criminals compared to street criminals.

The special sensitivity hypothesis assumes that the transition from a life of freedom and privilege to one of strict regulation and material deprivation may be particularly shocking to newly incarcerated white-collar inmates. The hypothesis implies that white-collar offenders have more to lose than other offenders by going to prison. The hypothesis considers as a extra burden the stigmatization experienced as a result of prestigious job loss, media coverage of the court case, asset recovery by the government, family breakup, reputation damage within the community, withdrawal of professional licenses, and dismissal from the elite. The hypothesis suggests that these circumstances far exceed what street criminals have to go through after detection and conviction (Logan 2015).

The idea that white-collar offenders are especially sensitive to the pains of imprisonment was developed with high-status offenders in mind. The idea stems from the fact that they differ substantially from other offenders with respect to their social and other background characteristics, as well as their experience of the criminal justice system (Logan 2015: 11):

> In light of these differences, members of the criminal justice community – namely judges – have argued that indoctrination to prison life is particularly shocking for newly incarcerated white-collar offenders. Similarly, these individuals maintain that typical street offenders, who often come from more disadvantaged backgrounds, are far less susceptible to the pains of imprisonment.

Stadler et al. (2013: 5) formulate the idea in a similar way, where the special sensitivity hypothesis is based on the undeniable fact that white-collar offenders are different from street offenders regarding their backgrounds:

> Because they would be transitioning from a life of freedom and privilege to a life with little or no liberty and possessions, incarceration is assumed to be especially shocking for white-collar offenders. In contrast, street offenders typically live more deprived lives and would therefore experience less of a culture shock upon incarceration.

Mann et al. (1979: 487) interviewed judges to explore their reasons and motivations for the special sensitivity hypothesis and got answers like the two following responses:

> A white-collar criminal has more of a fear of going to jail than this syndrome we find in the street crime. And I am not saying that if you cut everyone they don't bleed red blood. A person who commits a robbery or an assault, they don't want to go to jail either. But the white-collar criminal has more to lose by going to jail; reputation in community, business as well as social community, decent living conditions, just the whole business of being put in a prison with a number on his back demeans this tremendous ego that is always involved in people who are high achievers.
>
> It can be a major disruption for the family, for the individual. It may undermine his whole career. I can probably better understand the white-collar defendant. He is more like me and ... I guess I do believe that white-collar defendants are more sensitive to and more affected by the prison experience.

Defense attorneys are active supporters of the special sensitivity hypothesis. Their support comes as no surprise, since the magnitude of billable hours involved in white-collar defense far exceeds what is feasible in street crime defense. Often, attorneys are hired to contribute symbolic defense and information control, in addition to substance defense. They continue to work for their clients after conviction. Stadler et al. (2013: 18) found that:

> Almost without exception, defense attorneys argue that merely convicting a white-collar offender results in enough suffering. Prison, it is argued, would be an especially difficult hardship for these individuals because of their social background.

The special sensitivity hypothesis may seem particularly relevant in prison settings that are poorly managed and marked by high levels of inmate violence and other forms of victimization. In such environments, white-collar inmates can prove attractive targets and be neglected owing to lack of guardianship (Stadler et al. 2013).

References

Andersen, J. J., Johannesen, N., Lassen, D. D., & Paltseva, E. (2017). Petro Rents, Political Institutions, and Hidden Wealth: Evidence from Offshore Bank Accounts. *Journal of European Economic Association*, Volume 15, Issue 4, 1 August 2017, Pages 818–860. https://academic.oup.com/jeea/article-abstract/15/4/818/296561

Benson, M. L., & Simpson, S. S. (2015). *Understanding White-Collar Crime: An Opportunity Perspective*. New York: Routledge.

Bogen, T. (2008). *Hvor var du, historien om mitt liv* [Where Were You, the Story of My Life]. Oslo: Schibsted Publishing.

Croall, H. (1989). Who Is the White-Collar Criminal? *The British Journal of Criminology, 29*(2), 157–174.

Dearden, T. E. (2017). An Assessment of Adults' Views on White-Collar Crime. *Journal of Financial Crime, 24*(2), 309–321.

Dhami, M. K. (2007). White-Collar Prisoners' Perceptions of Audience Reaction. *Deviant Behavior, 28*, 57–77.

Eriksen, T. S. (2010). *Arven etter Ole Christian Bach – et justismord* [The Legacy of Ole Christian Bach – A Miscarriage of Justice]. Oslo: Norgesforlaget Publishing.

Fosse, G., & Magnusson, G. (2004). *Mayday Mayday! –Kapteinene først i livbåtene!* [Mayday Mayday! –The Captains First in the Lifeboats]. Oslo: Kolofon Publishing.

Green, S. P. (2007). *Lying, Cheating, and Stealing.* Oxford: Oxford University Press.

Kang, E., & Thosuwanchrot, N. (2017). An Application of Durkheim's Four Categories of Suicide to Organizational Crimes. *Deviant Behavior, 38*(5), 493–513.

Kerik, B. B. (2005). *From Jailer to Jailed – My Journey from Correction and Police Commissioner to Inmate #84888-054.* New York: Threshold Editions.

Leasure, P., & Zhang, G. (2017). "That's How They Taught Us to Do It": Learned Deviance and Inadequate Deterrents in Retail Banking. *Deviant Behavior.* Published online 28 February. https://doi.org/10.1080/01639625.2017.1286179.

Levi, M. (2002). Suite Justice or Sweet Charity? Some Explorations of Shaming and Incapacitating Business Fraudsters. *Punishment & Society, 4*(2), 147–163.

Logan, M. W (2015). *Coping with Imprisonment: Testing the Special Sensitivity Hypothesis for White-Collar Offenders.* A dissertation to the Graduate School of the University of Cincinnati in partial fulfilment of the requirements for the degree of Doctor of Philosophy in the Department of Criminal Justice, Cincinnati.

Mann, K., Wheeler, K., & Sarat, A. (1979). Sentencing the White Collar Defender. *American Criminal Law Review, 17,* 479–500.

Montella, E. C. (2016). *Full Circle: A Memoir of Leaning in Too Far and the Journey Back.* Sanibel: Triple M Press.

Naylor, R. T. (2003). Towards a General Theory of Profit-Driven Crimes. *British Journal of Criminology, 43,* 81–101.

Nelken, D. (2012). White-Collar and Corporate Crime. In M. Maguire, R. Morgan, & R. Reiner (Eds.), *The Oxford Handbook of Criminology.* Oxford: Oxford University Press.

Piquero, N. L., & Benson, M. L. (2004). White Collar Crime and Criminal Careers: Specifying a Trajectory of Punctuated Situational Offending. *Journal of Contemporary Criminal Justice, 20,* 148–165.

Pontell, H. N., Black, W. K., & Geis, G. (2014). Too Big to Fail, Too Powerful to Jail? On the Absence of Criminal Prosecutions After the 2008 Financial Meltdown. *Crime, Law and Social Change, 61*(1), 1–13.

Shapiro, S. P. (1987). The Social Control of Impersonal Trust. *American Journal of Sociology, 93*(3), 623–658.

Shover, N., Hochsteller, A., & Alalehto, T. (2012). Choosing White-Collar Crime. In F. T. Cullen & P. Wilcox (Eds.), *The Oxford Handbook of Criminological Theory.* Oxford: Oxford University Press.

Stadler, W. A., Benson, M. L., & Cullen, E. T. (2013). Revisiting the Special Sensitivity Hypothesis: The Prison Experience of White-Collar Inmates. *Justice Quarterly, 30*(6), 1090–1114.

Supernor, H. (2017). Community Service and White-Collar Offenders: The Characteristics of the Sanction on Factors Determining Its Use Among a Sample of Health-Care Offenders. *Journal of Financial Crime, 24*(1), 148–156.

Sutherland, E. H. (1939). White-Collar Criminality. *American Sociological Review, 5*, 1–12.

Sutherland, E. H. (1949). *White-Collar Crime.* New York: Holt, Rinehart and Winston Publishing.

Open Access This chapter is licensed under the terms of the Creative Commons Attribution 4.0 International License (http://creativecommons.org/licenses/by/4.0/), which permits use, sharing, adaptation, distribution and reproduction in any medium or format, as long as you give appropriate credit to the original author(s) and the source, provide a link to the Creative Commons license and indicate if changes were made.

The images or other third party material in this chapter are included in the chapter's Creative Commons license, unless indicated otherwise in a credit line to the material. If material is not included in the chapter's Creative Commons license and your intended use is not permitted by statutory regulation or exceeds the permitted use, you will need to obtain permission directly from the copyright holder.

CHAPTER 2

Theory of Crime Convenience

Abstract The theory of convenience attempts to integrate theoretical explanations for the occurrence of white-collar crime from sociology, psychology, management, organizational behavior, criminology, and other fields to shed light on different perspectives of convenience. Convenience can be both an absolute and a relative construct. As an absolute construct, it is attractive to commit financial crime as such. As a relative construct, it is more convenient to commit crime than to carry out alternative actions to solve a problem or gain benefits from an opportunity. White-collar criminals probably vary in their perceived convenience of their actions. Behavioral willingness can be high when the subjective detection risk is low. Detection risk is a combination of likelihood of detection and consequences after detection. Subjective detection risk varies among individuals.

Keywords Behavioral willingness • Convenience theory • Corporate hierarchy • Detection suicide • Deviant behavior • Expected utility • Financial motive • Organizational opportunity • Psychopathy • Self-control

Convenience theory suggests that white-collar criminals have a strong convenience orientation. The theory of convenience attempts to integrate various theoretical explanations for the occurrence of white-collar crime from sociology, psychology, management, organizational behavior, criminology,

© The Author(s) 2018
P. Gottschalk, L. Gunnesdal, *White-Collar Crime in the Shadow Economy*,
https://doi.org/10.1007/978-3-319-75292-1_2

and other related fields to shed light on the different perspectives of convenience. Convenience is a relative concept concerned with the efficiency of time and effort, as well as the reduction in pain and solution to problems (Engdahl 2015). Convenience orientation refers to a person's general preference for maneuvers characterized by the avoidance of pain and savings in time and effort. A convenience-oriented person is one who seeks to accomplish a task in the shortest time with the least expenditure of human energy. A convenient individual is not necessarily bad or lazy. On the contrary, the person can be seen as smart and rational in focusing the time and effort where it matters most for the individual or the organization (Sundström and Radon 2015).

Inmates with a strong convenience orientation favor actions and behaviors with inherent the characteristics of saving time and effort. They have a desire to spend as little time as possible on challenging issues and situations that may occur in prison. They have an attitude that the less effort needed the better, and they think that it will be a waste of time expending a long time on a problem. They prefer to avoid the problem rather than handle it, and want to avoid discomfort and pain. They want to survive prison life in the best possible way. Convenience motivates the choice of action and behavior, and an important element is avoiding more problematic, stressful, and challenging situations.

Convenience can be both an absolute construct and a relative construct. As an absolute construct, it is attractive to commit financial crime as such. As a relative construct, it is more convenient to commit crime than to carry out alternative actions to solve a problem or gain benefits from an opportunity. Convenience is an advantage in favor of a specific action to the detriment of alternative actions. Blickle et al. (2006) found that if the rationally expected utility of an action by a white-collar offender clearly outweighs the expected disadvantages resulting from the action, thereby leaving a net material advantage, then the offender will commit the offense in question.

In conclusion, the special sensitivity hypothesis often argued by white-collar defense attorneys and members of the elite finds little support in empirical studies of white-collar inmates versus street crime inmates. Instead, the special resilience hypothesis finds support, where white-collar inmates have the ability to adapt to prison life without much pain. The theory of convenience provides a basis for the special resilience hypothesis, because white-collar offenders tend to have a strong convenience orientation to avoid pain and the waste of energy.

White-collar crime can be a convenient option to avoid threats and exploit opportunities. Convenience is a concept that was theoretically mainly associated with efficiency in timesaving. Today, convenience is associated with a number of other characteristics, such as reduced effort and reduced pain, and with terms such as fast, easy, and safe. Finally, convenience says something about attractiveness and accessibility (Sundström and Radon 2015).

Convenience is characterized by comfortable practicality; it is simple and not necessarily bad or illegal. For example, ship-owners can register their boats under flags of convenience, which is to sail under false flags to reap economic benefits that might otherwise not be achievable. Convenience can be applying tricks of the trade without traces of obvious crime, lying in the gray zone, and exploiting the system for organizational or personal gain and pleasure. Convenience can be used to cause enrichment in an easy and comfortable manner without losing face or reputation (as long as the offender is not revealed). In academic research, some researchers use convenience samples, which consist of readily available respondents, for their empirical studies. The selection is not random and cannot be said to be representative of the population. It is unacceptable to generalize research results based on such convenience samples. Another example is the convenience store in terms of a grocery shop or a gas station, where consumer goods are easily available and accessible, but prices are higher and the selection is more limited (Sari et al. 2017).

Convenience orientation is the value that individuals and organizations place on actions with the inherent characteristics of saving time and effort. Convenience orientation is a value-like construct that influences behavior and decision-making. Mai and Olsen (2016) measured convenience orientation in terms of a desire to spend as little time as possible on the task, in terms of an attitude that the less effort needed the better, as well as in terms of a consideration that it is a waste of time to spend a long time on the task. Convenience orientation towards illegal actions increases as negative attitudes towards legal actions increase. The basic elements in convenience orientation are the executive attitudes towards the saving of time, effort, and discomfort in the planning, action, and achievement of goals. Generally, convenience orientation is the degree to which an executive is inclined to save time and effort to reach goals. Convenience orientation refers to a person's general preference for convenient maneuvers. A convenience-oriented person is one who seeks to accomplish a task in the shortest time with the least expenditure of human energy (Berry et al. 2002).

The actual convenience is not necessarily important in convenience theory. Rather, the perceived, expected, and assumed convenience influences the choice of action. Berry et al. (2002) make this distinction explicit by conceptualizing convenience as an individual's time and effort perceptions related to an action. White-collar criminals probably vary in their perceived convenience of their actions. Low expected convenience could be one of the reasons why not more members of the elite commit white-collar offenses.

Financial Motive

Threat of bankruptcy or threat of other kinds of financial loss is a frequent economical motive for white-collar crime. According to Piquero (2012), the fear of falling is strong among members of the elite. Kouchaki and Desai (2015: 362) found that the threat of falling may lead to unethical behavior:

> Perceived threat engenders self-protective defenses that cause people to focus narrowly on their own needs, which interfere with adherence to moral principles and encourage unethical acts.

Kouchaki and Desai (2015) suggest that people experiencing anxiety, nervousness, and worry are likely to behave selfishly and engage in self-interested unethical acts in an effort to restore the threatened self. Individuals experiencing threats tend to focus inward and acquire resources as a means of compensating for threats. In threatening situations, the brain tends to shift into a state that facilitates mobilization of defense mechanisms. Threats are typically characterized by the salience of risk of loss. Threats tend to bring about socially undesirable actions geared toward self-protection. To cope with threat, people rely on a variety of potential mechanisms to shield themselves from negative experiences and unpleasant feelings, and ultimately to protect their self-esteem.

Threats can create moral panic. Moral panic is used to characterize reactions that do not accurately reflect the actual danger of a threat. During a moral panic, sensitization processes generate an escalation in the individual disturbance (Kang and Thosuwanchot 2017).

Chattopadhyay et al. (2001) studied organizational actions in response to threats. They found that threats are associated with urgency, difficulty, and high stakes. Threats involve a negative situation in which loss is likely and over which one has relatively little control.

A possibility implies a positive situation in which gain is likely and over which one has a fair amount of control, while at the same time been characterized by urgency, difficulty, and high stakes (Chattopadhyay et al. 2001).

When an organization develops and maintains a strong systematic socialization program, employees not only identify with the organization but also its goals. When personal promotion or dismissal, as well as bonuses and benefits, are connected to the achievement of goals, then employees identify more strongly with organizational goals. When the socialization process is coupled with strong accountability systems, employees are regulated to achieve organizational goals. The pursuit of goals does not imply the absence of crime. The bottom-line focus in an organizational context might increase the frequency of financial crime on behalf of the organization for profit or enhancement. A strong emphasis on goal attainment might indeed lead organizational members to engage in illegal acts (Kang and Thosuwanchot 2017).

Kang and Thosuwanchot (2017: 501) recount the following story:

Philip R. Bennett joined Refco Inc. in 1981, becoming the chief financial officer (CFO) in 1983 and heading it as the chief executive officer (CEO) since 1998 following the retirement of Thomas Dittmer, the stepson of the company's founder. Bennett was asked to leave the company when federal prosecutors accused him of a "massive securities fraud, charging him with a scheme to hide a debt of as much as $545 million that he allegedly tried to keep secret from investors". In 2008, Bennett pleaded guilty to the charges and was sentenced to 16 years in prison.

Having been in Refco Inc. for more than 24 years and coupled with the helming of two high-ranking positions – CFO and ultimately CEO and chairman – Bennett's identification with the goals of Refco Inc. can be considered to be high. In other words, having spent sufficient time in a position of power in Refco Inc. with the ability to influence the company's direction, Bennett was highly socialized into the goals of the company.

One of Refco Inc's key goals was to go public to raise funds. The company engaged reputable institutions (i.e. Credit Suisse First Boston, Godman Sachs Group, and Bank of America Corp.) to underwrite its IPO in 2005. However, Bennett committed illegal acts to make Refco Inc. more attractive as an investment option in the public listing.

Organizational Opportunity

Those at the pinnacle of a corporate hierarchy (or just about any hierarchy, for that matter) who have considerable authority, are not often challenged, insist upon results, and are accustomed to getting their own way. Therefore, various forms of dishonest and illegal behavior that elite members are engaged in seem to be convenient for the offenders. They believe they can ignore various reservations they would have if they were lower down in the power structure, and if they were expected to demonstrate leadership and achieve ethical results. Greed, self-importance, immunity from criticism, getting one's own way, and fear of falling all contribute to the convenience of white-collar crime in the organizational setting. An offender is in a position to point to the importance of one's place in an organizational hierarchy, one's ability to cover one's tracks, blame others or insist on deniability, and the pressure to achieve results. White-collar criminals tend to engage in various rhetorical strategies to make it sound to their subordinates as though they have done nothing wrong.

Organizational dynamics is an interesting perspective on white-collar crime. Organizational dynamics can cause a downward spiral, leading to misconduct and crime. In the downward spiral, the tendency to commit white-collar crime increases. It becomes more convenient to commit crime in comparison to alternative actions when crises or opportunities emerge. Convenience theory suggests that white-collar crime can be an attractive option for executives and others in the elite. In this section, negative organizational dynamics is explained by institutional theory, social disorganization theory, slippery slope theory, neutralization theory, and differential association theory.

As argued by Ashkanasy et al. (2016), organizations are intrinsically human entities. Processes that drive human thought and behavior also drive organizations. If deviant behavior is preferred by some and accepted by others, then deviance may drive an organization. When a leader implicitly or explicitly defines misconduct and crime as acceptable, followers will tend to do the same. In the organizational setting, there is no organizational or corporate crime that is not driven by human thought and behavior.

The opportunity perspective is thus more than just an organization lacking control over its members. There are dynamics among members where some prefer convenient solutions to problems and challenges even when the solutions imply breaking the law. The organization is a community of practice where individuals merge into groups and departments to complete tasks and reach goals in ways that establish themselves over time through dynamic interactions between organizational members.

In their article on organizational dynamics to understand causes and effects of top management fraud, Zahra et al. (2007: 128) emphasize organization-level pressures:

> Without stockholder monitoring, some executives may act opportunistically and enrich themselves while foregoing stockholder-desired, long-term value creating activities for their firms.

Felson and Boba (2010) define white-collar crime as a crime of specialized access, where the offender is able to access resources by abusing routines in the organization.

BEHAVIORAL WILLINGNESS

Deviant behavior can be learned from others. In executive successions, cultural transmission tends to occur, for example from a retiring chief executive officer (CEO) to an emerging CEO. Cultural transmission can explain why individuals who were reluctant to adopt deviant behavior may engage in misconduct and crime. Cultural transmission models may explain the passing on of misconduct behavior in terms of white-collar crime. Generally, such models explain the transfer of cultural norms, values, and belief systems that are transmitted between individuals or groups within and across generations. Transmission of criminal behavior across generations of executives occurs via a learning process with predecessors as well as in delinquent associations and peers. The principles of cultural transmission and differential association can be applied to corporate offending.

The concept of deviance is here an attribute of individuals, where we focus on negative forms of deviance in terms of white-collar crime within organizational contexts. Deviance is non-conformance to a norm that refers to any type of behavior that fails to meet normative standards and that may evoke a collective response of a negative type. Negative deviance is intentional behavior that departs from the norms of a referent group in bad ways (Mertens et al. 2016).

Deviance is here both behavior and outcome as behavior leads to crime. It is a departure from organizational norms in legal organizations, where organizational norms are informal or formal rules that regulate bandwidths and boundaries for behavior (Mertens et al. 2016).

Craig and Piquero (2017) studied two personality traits that sometimes predict offending intentions. Low self-control and desire-for-control are two personality traits that can have multiple effects on white-collar offending. Findings suggest that while low self-control was predictive of intention to offend, the impact of desire-for-control varied based on the respondent's level of self-control. In contrast to prior studies, desire-for-control reduced offending intentions, but only among those with high self-control.

Self-control reflects an individual's capacity and motivation to override desires and urges in order to act in accordance with one's norms and goals, such as maintaining positive relationships with others. Soltes (2016: 54) suggests that "people with lower self-control have greater difficulty resisting temptation and restraining reckless behavior, and eventually some of this rash and opportunistic behavior is likely to end up as criminal conduct".

Liang et al. (2016) argue that effective human functioning requires the capacity to transcend primal desires and habitual behaviors in order to behave in a socially appropriate manner. When self-control fails, individuals disregard the long-term implications of their behaviors and succumb to their desires, such as cheating and bribing.

Liang et al. (2016: 1388) suggest that self-control is determined by two forces:

> The first is a primitive impulsive system wherein desire arises and drives behaviors, and the second is a higher-order reflective system wherein the desires and action tendencies that arise in the first primitive impulsive system are monitored and restrained.

White-collar offenders rationalize their own misconduct: Misconduct through which they sought fast, desirable results by violating the rules but they expected to be able to get away with it.

Behavioral willingness can be high when the subjective detection risk is low. Detection risk is a combination of likelihood of detection and consequences after detection. Subjective detection risk varies among individuals and is influenced by a number of factors.

Attitudes towards police performance or effectiveness are one such factor. When white-collar offenders believe that the police are unable to solve crime, then the risk of criminal behavior is low. The police do not operate in a vacuum. They rely on community members to report crime, serve as witnesses in court, and act as capable guardians over people and property.

As such, police effectiveness is also based on the level of support that the community provides to the police. Policing practice reveals that businesses that have suffered from financial crime have lower trust in, confidence in, and satisfaction with, law enforcement. Hence, the legitimacy of the police is often rooted in the level of corporate support that they receive. As such, confidence in the police may actually impact levels of white-collar crime within private and public organizations.

On the other hand, collective efficacy in law enforcement may increase subjective detection risk. Collective efficacy holds that organizational members and stakeholders work collectively toward a common objective, such as crime control and maintenance of order. The fundamental component of collective efficacy is the notion of social trust amongst all actors working towards a common goal. All members of the relevant communities work together to control crime through mutual trust. However, when trust or confidence in the police is lacking or non-existent, the possibility of reducing actual levels of crime will be diminished.

Some white-collar criminals suffer from personality disorders such as psychopathy. Psychopathy can be characterized by fearlessness, antisocial behavior combined with high social attention seeking, immunity to stress, egoism, and self-centered impulsivity.

The behavioral willingness to commit white-collar crime can be reversed when fraud is detected. Especially in cases of personality disorder, a possible outcome is detection suicide. Brody and Perri (2016: 786) recount the following story:

> To outsiders, Darrin Campbell was the picture of an unassuming prosperous executive. However, records show that Campbell was at the center of a securities fraud scandal that accompanied the collapse of Tampa-based Anchor Glass Container Corporation, then the third-largest manufacturer of glass containers in the USA. Shareholders accused him and other executives of failing to disclose financial weaknesses before a public stock offering, leading to lawsuits and a multimillion-dollar settlement. As part of the settlement, Campbell did not have to admit wrongdoing. Yet, after this incident, there were speculations that perhaps Campbell and his family were having financial problems. Campbell can be seen purchasing items that he would eventually use to kill and burn their home with. Campbell, with a handgun, eventually executed his 51-year-old wife, his 18-year-old son and 15-year-old daughter before burning down the family's home and shooting himself in the head. What transformed a 49-year-old executive into a methodical killer who eventually committed suicide?

Brody and Perri (2016) reflect on this question by discussing negative life events as a major cause of most suicides. Similarly, Kang and Thosuwanchot (2017) describe four categories of suicide that all have the aspects of negative life events for white-collar offenders. First, egoistic suicide is filled with apathy, indolent melancholy with complacence. Second, altruistic suicide is filled with energy of passion or will, with calm feeling of duty, mystic enthusiasm, or peaceful courage. Third, anomic suicide is filled with irritation or disgust, with violent recriminations against life in general or against one particular person. Fourth, fatalistic suicide is derived from excessive regulation, that of persons with futures pitilessly blocked and passions violently choked by oppressive discipline.

Personality disorder is characterized as enduring maladaptive patterns of behavior and experience involving at least two of the following four areas: Cognitive, affective, interpersonal, and/or control of impulse.

REFERENCES

Ashkanasy, N. M. (2016). Why We Need Theory in the Organization Sciences. *Journal of Organizational Behavior, 37*(8), 1126–1131.

Berry, L. L., Seiders, K., & Grewal, D. (2002). Understanding Service Convenience. *Journal of Marketing, 66*, 1–17.

Blickle, G., Schlegel, A., Fassbender, P., & Klein, U. (2006). Some Personality Correlates of Business White-Collar Crime. *Applied Psychology: An International Review, 55*(2), 220–233.

Brody, R. G., & Perri, F. S. (2016). Fraud Detection Suicide: The Dark Side of White-Collar Crime. *Journal of Financial Crime, 23*(4), 786–797.

Chattopadhyay, P., Glick, W. H., & Huber, G. P. (2001). Organizational Actions in Response to Threats and Opportunities. *Academy of Management Journal, 44*(5), 937–955.

Craig, J. M., & Piquero, N. L. (2017). The Effects of Low Self-Control and Desire-for-Control on White-Collar Offending: A Replication. *Deviant Behavior, 37*(11), 1308–1324.

Engdahl, O. (2015). White-Collar Crime and First-Time Adult-Onset Offending: Explorations in the Concept of Negative Life Events as Turning Points. *International Journal of Law, Crime and Justice, 43*(1), 1–16.

Felson, M., & Boba, R. L. (2010). *Crime and Everyday Life*, Chapter 12: "White-Collar Crime". Thousand Oaks: Sage Publications.

Kang, E., & Thosuwanchot, N. (2017). An Application of Durkheim's Four Categories of Suicide to Organizational Crimes. *Deviant Behavior, 38*(5), 493–513.

Kouchaki, M., & Desai, S. D. (2015). Anxious, Threatened, and Also Unethical: How Anxiety Makes Individuals Feel Threatened and Commit Unethical Acts. *Journal of Applied Psychology, 100*(2), 360–375.

Liang, L. H., Lian, H., Brown, D. J., Ferris, D. L., Hanig, S., & Keepoing, L. M. (2016). Why Are Abusive Supervisors Abusive? A Dual-System Self-Control Model. *Academy of Management Journal, 59*(4), 1385–1406.

Mai, H. T. X., & Olsen, S. O. (2016). Consumer Participation in Self-Production: The Role of Control Mechanisms, Convenience Orientation, and Moral Obligation. *Journal of Marketing Theory and Practice, 24*(2), 209–223.

Mertens, W., Recker, J., Kohlborn, T., & Kummer, T. F. (2016). A Framework for the Study of Positive Deviance in Organizations. *Deviant Behavior, 37*(11), 1288–1307.

Piquero, N. L. (2012). The Only Thing We Have to Fear Is Fear Itself: Investigating the Relationship Between Fear of Falling and White Collar Crime. *Crime and Delinquency, 58*(3), 362–379.

Sari, Y. K., Shaari, Z. H., & Amar, A. B. (2017). Measurement Development of Customer Patronage of Petrol Station with Convenience Store. *Global Business and Management Research: An International Journal, 9*(1), 52–62.

Soltes, E. (2016). *Why They Do It: Inside the Mind of the White-Collar Criminal.* New York: Public Affairs Books.

Sundström, M., & Radon, A. (2015). Utilizing the Concept of Convenience as a Business Opportunity in Emerging Markets. *Organizations and Markets in Emerging Economies, 6*(2), 7–21.

Zahra, S. A., Priem, R. L., & Rasheed, A. A. (2007). Understanding the Causes and Effects of Top Management Fraud. *Organizational Dynamics, 36*(2), 122–139.

Open Access This chapter is licensed under the terms of the Creative Commons Attribution 4.0 International License (http://creativecommons.org/licenses/by/4.0/), which permits use, sharing, adaptation, distribution and reproduction in any medium or format, as long as you give appropriate credit to the original author(s) and the source, provide a link to the Creative Commons license and indicate if changes were made.

The images or other third party material in this chapter are included in the chapter's Creative Commons license, unless indicated otherwise in a credit line to the material. If material is not included in the chapter's Creative Commons license and your intended use is not permitted by statutory regulation or exceeds the permitted use, you will need to obtain permission directly from the copyright holder.

CHAPTER 3

Tip of the Crime Iceberg

Abstract We apply the method of expert elicitation to estimate the size of the iceberg and to evaluate reasons why so few white-collar criminals are convicted. We address the following research questions: What is the estimated magnitude of white-collar crime? Why are many white-collar criminals never detected, investigated, prosecuted, and convicted? From our database, we know that 58 white-collar criminals were sentenced to prison every year between 2009 and 2015 in Norway, and we know the average amount involved in their crime. Based on this knowledge, is it possible to estimate the total magnitude of white-collar crime in the country? We recruited a panel of 15 experts to estimate a number of parameters that can determine the total amount of money lost yearly because of white-collar crime.

Keywords Categories of crime • Categories of victims • Criminal level • Diversity of participants • Empirical sample • Expert elicitation • Expert judgment inference • Gender • Magnitude of crime • Sources of detection

It is often argued that detected and convicted white-collar criminals only represent the tip of an iceberg in terms of financial crime committed by privileged people in the elite linked to their occupations in society (Langton and Piquero 2007). Ever since Sutherland (1939) coined the term white-collar crime, researchers have studied characteristics of white-collar criminals such as their financial motives, their organizational opportunities, and their deviant behaviors. These three dimensions can be integrated into convenience theory as a general explanation of the white-collar crime phenomenon.

However, little is known about the magnitude of white-collar crime.

In this book, we apply the method of expert elicitation to estimate the size of the iceberg and to evaluate reasons why so few white-collar criminals are convicted. We address the following research questions: What is the estimated magnitude of white-collar crime? Why are many white-collar criminals never detected, investigated, prosecuted and convicted?

Empirical Sample of Criminals

From our database, we know that, on average, 58 white-collar criminals were sentenced to prison in Norway every year between 2009 and 2015, and we know the average amount involved in their crime (19 million NOK). The total crime adjusted to 2015 prices thus amounts to 1.137 billion NOK.

Based on this knowledge, is it possible to estimate the total magnitude of white-collar crime in the country? We recruited an expert panel to estimate a number of parameters that could determine the total amount of money lost annually because of white-collar crime. Several estimation approaches were applied in the expert panel: Total dark (i.e., hidden) figure, groups of offenders, groups of offences, groups of victims, gender, and estimates of total crime.

White-collar criminals can be classified into three categories. First, at the top level, we find criminals such as executives and attorneys. Next, at the middle level, we find criminals such as investors and accounting managers. Finally, at the basic level, we find criminals such as accounting clerks and carpenters. In the total sample of 405 convicted white-collar criminals in Norway from 2009 to 2015, there are 28.4 percent in category 1, 46.1 percent in category 2 and 25.5 percent in category 3. The amount of money involved in the top level group is much bigger than in group 2, which is again bigger than group 3 (i.e., 33.0 million, 16.6 million and 9.7 million).

Another way of classifying white-collar crime is into crime categories. We make distinctions between four main categories of crime:

- Fraud: The intentional perversion of truth for the purpose of inducing another in reliance upon it to part with some valuable thing belonging to him or to surrender a legal right. Example: False documents to achieve bank financing.

- Theft: The illegal taking of another person's, group's, or organization's property without the victim's consent. Example: Executive takes corporate art works home.
- Manipulation: The means of gaining illegal control or influence over others' activities, means, and results. Example: Accounting misrepresentation to achieve tax evasion.
- Corruption: The giving, requesting, receiving, or accepting of an improper advantage related to a position, office, or assignment. Example: Procurement executive receives a bribe from a vendor.

In the sample of 405 convicts, 42.6 percent committed fraud, 4.2 percent committed theft, 35.3 percent committed manipulation, and 17.9 percent committed corruption. In cases of fraud, the average amount of money involved is much larger than in the other categories. In fraud cases, the average amount was 25.4 million NOK, in theft cases 4.8 million NOK, in manipulation cases 22.8 million NOK, and in corruption cases 2.5 million NOK.

A third way of classifying white-collar crime is according to categories of victims. We know that 27.9 percent victimized their employers, 22.1 percent victimized the internal revenue service (the Norwegian Tax Administration), 16.4 percent victimized customers, 14.2 percent victimized banks, and 7.4 percent victimized shareholders, while 12.0 percent victimized others. The amount of money involved in crime is larger for bank fraud, insider trading, and tax evasion than for crime against employers, customers, and shareholders. Bank fraud amounts to 49.5 million NOK on average, while insider trading hurting shareholders amounts to 29.8 million NOK, tax evasion 18 million NOK, customer fraud 17.3 million NOK, employee fraud 8.7 million NOK, and others 6.9 million NOK.

A fourth categorization is gender in terms of female versus male criminals. Among the convicts, 7.6 percent were women, while 92.4 percent were men. The average amount of money involved in crime was much larger for male than for female offenders: 20.4 million NOK versus 9.0 million NOK.

These breakdowns in our empirical sample enable experts to indicate a number of probabilities for the iceberg depending on criminal level, criminal type, victim group, and gender. Our ambition as researchers was to apply a number of these breakdowns to arrive at sound estimates from each expert and then accumulate those estimates for all experts.

In addition to different breakdowns, we also wanted estimates in terms of both an overall and a probability distribution of an estimate of the fraction of white-collar criminals that are caught and brought to justice, in addition to an estimate of the total amount of money involved. Thus, we have a total of seven approaches to estimate the magnitude of white-collar crime:

1. Fraction of white-collar criminals that are caught and brought to justice
2. Fraction with a probability distribution of white-collar criminals that are caught and brought to justice
3. Fraction of white-collar offender groups that are caught and brought to justice
4. Fraction of white-collar crime categories that are detected and lead to conviction
5. Fraction of white-collar crime victim groups that lead to detection and conviction
6. Fraction of white-collar male and female offenders that are caught and brought to justice
7. Total magnitude of white-collar crime in billions of NOK.

We also make distinctions between: (i) white-collar criminals never detected; (ii) white-collar criminals detected, but never investigated; (iii) white collar criminals detected and investigated, but never prosecuted; and (iv) white-collar criminals detected, investigated, and prosecuted, but not sentenced. In all four categories, it is assumed that the offenders are guilty. This research is important in the context of business continuity and risk management, as the iceberg is a threat to business and the number of white-collar criminals never detected is a challenge for risk managers. Furthermore, lack of detection increases the attraction to commit white-collar crime.

Expert Elicitation

One approach to estimate the size of the iceberg is the use of expert elicitation. Expert elicitation refers to a systematic approach to synthesize subjective judgments of experts on a topic where there is uncertainty due to lack of data (Heyman and Sailors 2016; Valkenhoef and Tervonen 2016).

The purpose of eliciting and analyzing expert judgment is to use all available information to make expert judgment inference, which is different from statistical inference. Statistical inference means that conclusions about the population can be established when the sample is randomly drawn for the population. Expert judgment inference means that experts' estimates represent the state of knowledge. It represents previously unknown and undocumented information. The limited ability to infer does not mean that expert judgments are not valid data. Expert judgments are indeed valid data in that they must be carefully gathered, analyzed, and interpreted (Meyer and Booker 2001).When a number of experts are interviewed, their accumulated guesstimates tend to converge towards numbers that remain stable when more experts are added. Therefore, approximately ten experts from various backgrounds are often sufficient (Heyman and Sailors 2016; Slottje et al. 2008: 7; Valkenhoef and Tervonen 2016).

Expert elicitation seeks to make explicit and utilizable the unpublished knowledge and wisdom in the heads of experts, based on their accumulated experience as well as their interpretation and reflection in a given context. It is a systematic approach that includes expert insights into the subject and also insights into the limitations, strengths, and weaknesses of published studies (Slottje et al. 2008: 7):

> Usually the subjective judgment is represented as a 'subjective' probability density function (PDF) reflecting the experts' belief regarding the quantity at hand, but it can also be for instance the experts' beliefs regarding the shape of a given exposure response function. An expert elicitation procedure should be developed in such a way that minimizes biases in subjective judgment and errors related to that in the elicited outcomes.

Meyer and Booker (2001) argue that expert elicitation is invaluable for assessing products, systems, and situations for which measurements or test results are sparse or non-existent. When experts disagree, it can mean that they interpreted the question differently or that they solved it using different lines of thought. Expert judgment can be considered relevant information in the sense that it is data based on qualified opinions. The validity or quality of expert judgment, like any data, can vary. The quality of expert judgment depends on both the completeness of the expert's mental model of the phenomena in question and the process used to elicit, model, analyze, and interpret the data.

In Scandinavia, expert elicitation has been applied to estimate the magnitude of social security fraud. While the estimate for Sweden was 6–7 percent (Delegationen 2008), the estimate for Norway was 5 percent (Proba 2013). Slottje et al. (2008) applied expert elicitation in the Netherlands to assess environmental health impact.

Expert elicitation faces some of the same challenges as elite interviewing, where there are issues associated with anonymity and confidentiality produced through power relations between researcher and participant (Lancaster 2017). Expert elicitation shares similarities with expert provocation, where critical reflection is stimulated amongst participants on issues that are often otherwise overlooked (Pangrazio 2017).

Through systematic interviews of experts, we tried to estimate the magnitude of white-collar crime in Norway. On our way to a final answer, we were faced with a number of obstacles in our research design. A later chapter explains our research journey by communicating our learning from methodological challenges when applying expert elicitation to estimate the size of an iceberg based on knowledge about the tip of the iceberg. In particular, participation refusals and response confusions are discussed.

Expert Panel

In expert elicitation, an early methodological step involves identification of experts in the subject area. An expert is anyone especially knowledgeable in the field and at the level of detail being elicited. Meyer and Booker (2001) distinguish between two types of expertise: Substantive and normative. Substantive expertise comes from the expert's experience in the field in question. Normative expertise is knowledge related to the use of the response mode. The response mode is the form in which the expert is asked to give a judgment.

We define experts to be persons who have contributed to detection of white-collar crime. In the sample of 405 convicts, we identified the sources of detection as follows:

- Journalists detected 101 offenders (25 percent).
- Victims detected 52 offenders (13 percent).
- Bankruptcy auditors detected 45 offenders (11 percent).
- Internal auditors detected 45 offenders (11 percent).
- Tax administration employees detected 25 offenders (6 percent).
- Bank clerks detected 18 offenders (4 percent).
- External auditors detected 18 offenders (4 percent).
- Police officers detected 9 offenders (2 percent).
- Stock exchange employees detected 4 offenders (1 percent).
- Others detected 88 offenders (23 percent).

It is a diverse range of experts, as recommended by Meyer and Booker (2001), so that the problem of estimating the magnitude is likely to be thoroughly considered from many viewpoints. Diversity of participants is one way to minimize the influence of a single individual. Some of these categories, however, are not relevant or feasible. For example, while a victim of white-collar crime has a strong memory of the episode, there is only one episode, from which the victim as a respondent can hardly generalize.

We developed a questionnaire for the experts and applied the survey in two steps. First, an email was sent to experts informing them about the attached questionnaire and telling them that they would be contacted for a phone interview by a researcher a few days later. During the phone interview, experts had the opportunity to ask the researcher for clarification and discuss issues. While they were talking on the phone, the researcher filled in the questionnaire based on the responses from the expert. The combination of mail and phone as two different communication channels is considered a feasible response mode in line with normative expertise.

We obtained responses in interviews from 15 experts as listed in Table 3.1. On average, the panel reported to have 16 years of experience working with financial crime.

Table 3.1 White-collar crime experts on the elicitation research panel

Category	Number
Investigative journalist in major newspaper	1
Experienced bankruptcy attorney	1
Experienced internal auditor	1
Tax administration fraud investigators	3
Investigative bank manager	2
Police detective	1
Corruption researcher	1
Private fraud examiners	2
Corporate investor	1
Defense attorney	1
Social security fraud investigator	1
Total respondents	15

The expert panel listed in Table 3.1 is not perfect, as we would have liked an even closer match to the sources of detection as previously listed. For example, we would have preferred more investigative journalists.

REFERENCES

Delegationen. (2008). *Vad koster felen? Omfattning av felaktiga utbetalingar från trygghetssystemen* [What Does the Mistake Cost? Estimation of Wrongful Payments from the Security System]. Stockholm: Delegationen mot felaktiga utbetalningar.

Heyman, J., & Sailors, J. (2016). A Respondent-Friendly Method of Ranking Long Lists. *International Journal of Market Research, 58*(5), 693–710.

Lancaster, K. (2017). Confidentiality, Anonymity and Power Relations in Elite Interviewing: Conducting Quality Policy Research in a Politicized Domain. *International Journal of Social Research Methodology, 20*(1), 93–103.

Langton, L., & Piquero, N. L. (2007). Can General Strain Theory Explain White-Collar Crime? A Preliminary Investigation of the Relationship Between Strain and Select White-Collar Offenses. *Journal of Criminal Justice, 35*, 1–15.

Meyer, M. A., & Booker, J. M. (2001). *Eliciting and Analyzing Expert Judgment: A Practical Guide, SIAM Books, ASA-SIAM Series on Statistics and Applied Probability*. Philadelphia: Society for Industrial and Applied Mathematics (SIAM).

Pangrazio, L. (2017). Exploring Provocation as a Research Method in the Social Sciences. *International Journal of Social Research Methodology*. Published online https://doi.org/10.1080/13645579.2016.1161346.

Proba. (2013). *Trygdesvindel i Norge: En kartlegging av fem stønadsordninger* [Social Security Fraud in Norway: A Survey of Five Support Areas]. Oslo: Proba samfunnsanalyse.

Slottje, P., Sluijs, J. P., & Knol, A. B. (2008). *Expert Elicitation: Methodological Suggestions for Its Use in Environmental Health Impact Assessments* (RIVM Letter Report). The Netherlands: National Institute for Public Health and the Environment.

Sutherland, E. H. (1939). White-Collar Criminality. *American Sociological Review, 5*, 1–12.

Valkenhoef, G., & Tervonen, T. (2016). Entropy-Optimal Weight Constraint Elicitation with Additive Multi-attribute Utility Models. *Omega, 64*, 1–12.

Open Access This chapter is licensed under the terms of the Creative Commons Attribution 4.0 International License (http://creativecommons.org/licenses/by/4.0/), which permits use, sharing, adaptation, distribution and reproduction in any medium or format, as long as you give appropriate credit to the original author(s) and the source, provide a link to the Creative Commons license and indicate if changes were made.

The images or other third party material in this chapter are included in the chapter's Creative Commons license, unless indicated otherwise in a credit line to the material. If material is not included in the chapter's Creative Commons license and your intended use is not permitted by statutory regulation or exceeds the permitted use, you will need to obtain permission directly from the copyright holder.

CHAPTER 4

Expert Elicitation for Estimation

Abstract In 2015, the head of the National Authority for Investigation and Prosecution of Economic and Environmental Crime (Økokrim), Trond Eirik Schea, estimated that as many as three out of every four white-collar criminals went unpunished in Norway. We use a total of seven approaches to estimate the magnitude of white-collar crime. According to our experts, the most likely estimate is 11.9 billion NOK (the average estimate from our seven approaches). Our low estimate of 4.4 billion NOK per year roughly translates into three out of four white-collar criminals getting away every year. This equals Schea's estimate. Our experts, however, claim that there is a 90 percent probability that this figure is too low, and that the problem we are facing is in fact larger.

Keywords Average amount • Estimation approaches • Fraction detected and convicted • Probability distribution • Size of the iceberg • Trond Eirik Schea • Type of crime • Type of offender • US estimates • Uncertainty

In 2015, the head of the National Authority for Investigation and Prosecution of Economic and Environmental Crime (Økokrim), Trond Eirik Schea, told the Norwegian newspaper *Dagens Næringsliv* that probably as many as three out of every four white-collar criminals went unpunished in

Norway. At the same time, he admitted that the probability of getting caught should be larger. How reasonable is Schea's benchmark estimate that only one out of four criminals are caught and brought to justice?

As noted above, we have a total of seven approaches to estimating the magnitude of white-collar crime:

1. Fraction of white-collar criminals that are caught and brought to justice.
2. Fraction with a probability distribution of white-collar criminals that are caught and brought to justice.
3. Fraction of white-collar offender groups that are caught and brought to justice.
4. Fraction of white-collar crime categories that are detected and lead to conviction.
5. Fraction of white-collar crime victim groups that lead to detection and conviction.
6. Fraction of white-collar male and female offenders that are caught and brought to justice.
7. Total magnitude of white-collar crime in billions of NOK.

Fraction of White-Collar Criminals

We first asked our experts the following question: How large a fraction of all white-collar criminals that commit financial crime in this country do you think are detected and imprisoned? The average answer (excluding the experts with the highest and the lowest estimates) was 9.4 percent or that about one out of ten are caught and sentenced.

To arrive at an estimate of what this implied for the total size of white-collar crime, we also asked our experts for their opinion on the relative size of the amounts involved in undetected versus detected crimes. If they, for instance, thought that most big-time criminals were indeed among the small proportion of criminals that were caught and convicted, then the size of our iceberg would be relatively small. And conversely, if they thought that the convicted mostly represented relatively small players, then we could have assumed that the size of the iceberg was even larger than the share of convicted criminals would imply.

On average, the experts believe that the undetected criminals represent crimes that are slightly bigger in money terms than detected crimes.

In other words, they believe the convicted criminals are slightly smaller fish in the sea of crime. Seven out of 15 experts said that above average amounts were probably hidden in legal cases that had not ended in convictions. Three experts argued that there is no difference. Five experts indicated that bigger fish are convicted. On average, the panel of experts is of the opinion that the average amount of money involved is 11.9 percent higher for the 90.6 percent of offenders who are never brought to justice. Our estimate for the total amount of white-collar crime is therefore multiplied by a factor of 1.108 (0.094 + 0.906 × 1.119).

Given our assumptions, 1.1 billion NOK representing 9.4 percent convicted criminals results in an estimated magnitude of 13.4 billion NOK in white-collar crime. This result is computed as follows: 1137 million × 1.108 × (100/9.4) = 13,402 million NOK.

Fraction with Probability Distribution

Based on what percentage the experts suggested in question 1, respondents were faced with nine intervals, where we asked them to place a total of 100 percentage points. When experts were asked for a probability distribution rather than one single percentage, this yielded similar results. The average of all distributions was 10.2 percent detection and conviction. This resulted in an estimate of white-collar crime magnitude of 12.3 billion NOK.

Our respondents varied in the extent to which they wanted to spread their estimate. Two placed all percentage points at one place on the scale as they did not want to indicate uncertainty. Others wanted to spread small probabilities across relatively large intervals. Four experts provided a lower percentage estimate with weighting than without. Two reported the same, and nine experts provided a weighted estimate for the conviction rate that was higher than the initial estimate at question 1, and thus a smaller iceberg size.

It is certainly difficult to create such a probability distribution, and there were some experts who found this question challenging. Some respondents were not quite aware of how much it affected the weighted estimate to add small probabilities at high percentages. This may have contributed to some experts' weighted estimates being higher than their answer to question 1, even though they explicitly said during the interview that they thought it was more likely that the percentage was lower than it was higher. For example, one expert stated that his choice to estimate 5 percent in question 1 was probably optimistic, and he could well have said 3 percent. Nevertheless, his weighted estimate ended above 7 percent.

Answers that we received to this question can be summarized in Fig. 4.1. The figure illustrates that there are differing opinions among experts concerning the fraction of white-collar criminals that are brought to justice every year.

While the two experts with the highest and lowest weighted estimate were excluded, the remaining panel thought it was most likely that the population convicted ranged between 2.5 percent and 5 percent. The experts also believed that it was equally likely that the population convicted was less than 2.5 percent of the total population of white-collar criminals than that it was above 20 percent. Overall, they thought there was a 65 percent probability that the percentage actually convicted was lower than the average estimate of about 10 percent. As a group, our panel thus believes that it is almost twice as likely that the total amount is greater than the roughly 12 billion NOK they estimated on average, than that the amount is less.

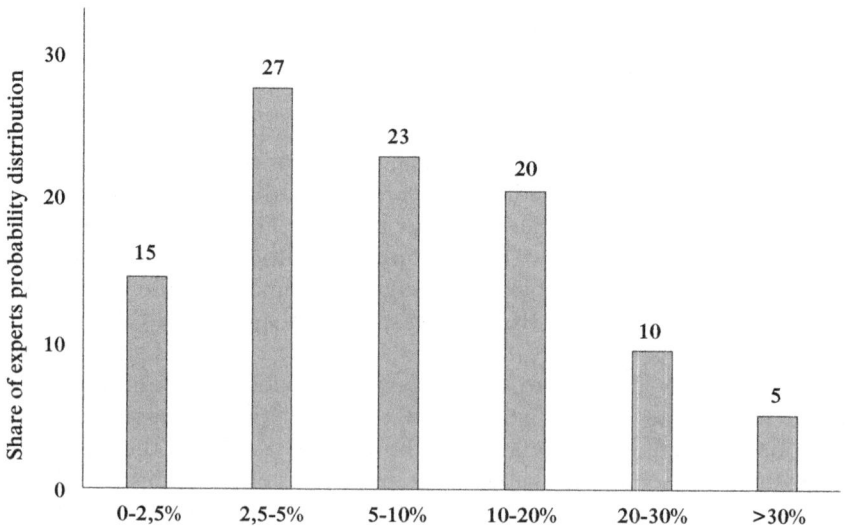

Fig. 4.1 Fraction of white-collar criminals that are brought to justice

Table 4.1 Estimation based on levels of white-collar criminals

Approach 3: Type of white-collar offender

Level of white-collar criminals	Figures from our database		Expert panel's estimate	
	Fraction of population (%)	Crime amount (million NOK)	Fraction convicted (%)	Sum of money (billion NOK)
Top level	28.4	33.0	8.5	7.1
Middle level	46.1	16.6	10.8	4.6
Basic level	25.5	9.7	12.8	1.3
Total	100			12.9

FRACTION OF OFFENDER GROUPS

Three levels of offenders were defined in this research: (i) top level offenders such as executives and attorneys, (ii) middle level offenders such as investors and accounting managers, and (iii) basic level offenders such as accounting clerks and carpenters. As listed in Table 4.1, respondents believe the fraction of convictions is lower among top level offenders. This approach resulted in an estimate of white-collar crime being in the magnitude of 12.9 billion NOK.

Respondents indicate in Table 4.1 that the position in the hierarchy of white-collar criminals influences the extent of conviction of white-collar crime. The lowest conviction rate is among the top level criminals who are abusing large sums of money. "Chief financial officers get more easily off the hook, than accountants", one expert said. Several experts said, for example, that very few attorneys are convicted. "Lawyers are very difficult to catch because of confidentiality in the client-attorney relationship, there might have been uncovered much more", another expert said. Yet another expert pointed out that higher up the ladder, an offender is much more capable of covering his or her criminal tracks, and the offender has better access to resources for defense in case of litigation. "Lawyers and CFOs have several tools at their disposal", the expert added.

FRACTION OF CRIME CATEGORIES

Distinction is made between fraud, theft, manipulation, and corruption. As listed in Table 4.2, experts believe theft is most often detected and convicted. Experts believe that corruption most seldom leads to conviction. One reason might be that both parties to the crime—the briber and

Table 4.2 Estimation based on categories of white-collar crime

Approach 4: Type of white-collar crime

	Figures from our database		Expert panel's estimate	
Category of white-collar crime	Fraction of population (%)	Crime amount (million NOK)	Fraction convicted (%)	Sum of money (billion NOK)
Fraud	42.6	25.4	12.4	5.6
Theft	4.2	4.8	16.9	0.1
Manipulation	35.3	22.8	9.4	5.5
Corruption	17.9	2.5	5.7	0.5
Total	100			11.8

the bribed—are best served by never disclosing their criminal act. This approach resulted in an estimate of the magnitude of white-collar crime of 11.7 billion NOK.

One expert commented on the low conviction fractions for manipulation and corruption: "There are many blurred lines in manipulation and corruption. I think many people do as they always have done, with the attitude that 'it must surely be okay'. Fraud and theft are much more clear-cut, everyone understands that it is wrong. That is why the dark figures are not equally large for those two categories."

Fraction of Victim Groups

Distinction is made between the following groups of victims: Employers, banks, the tax service, customers, shareholders, and others. As listed in Table 4.3, experts believe bank fraud, tax evasion, and employee fraud achieves a higher conviction rate than customer fraud, insider trading, and cases with other victims. This approach resulted in an estimate of the magnitude of white-collar crime of 10.6 billion NOK.

Several respondents felt that large employers and banks have good control over their capital flows, and that they have the muscle to clean up misconduct cases internally. Rather than "making noise" by reporting their employees to the police, such organizations prefer to offer severance packages to people so that they leave quietly, one respondent said. Many businesses do not like to lose face, another said: "Many companies have no desire to end up on a newspaper front page telling they have unfaithful servants in their ranks."

Table 4.3 Estimation based on categories of white-collar crime victims

Approach 5: Type of victim

Category of white-collar crime victim	Figures from our database		Expert panel's estimate	
	Fraction of population (%)	Crime amount (million NOK)	Fraction convicted (%)	Sum of money (billion NOK)
Employers	27.9	8.7	13.4	1.2
Banks	14.2	49.5	14.9	3.0
Tax authority	22.1	18.0	14.2	1.9
Customers	16.4	17.3	8.6	2.1
Shareholders	7.4	29.8	8.2	1.7
Others	12.0	6.9	8.6	0.6
Total	100			10.6

GENDER FRACTIONS

Only 7.6 percent of convicted white-collar criminals in Norway are women, while 92.4 percent are men. Perhaps the rate of detection and conviction is dependent on gender. Our experts think so, as shown in Table 4.4, where respondents believe that only 6.5 percent of female white-collar criminals are caught and brought to justice. This approach resulted in an estimate of the magnitude of white-collar crime of 12.2 billion NOK.

The average man's crime amount is more than twice as large as for female offenders. One explanation for this difference, experts said, is owing to the difference in positions held by men and women in organizations. "Men are often in key positions, and closer to the money", one expert said. Several experts gave the impression that it is "easier" to be a female criminal, because females get away with it more easily, since they are not suspected of crime. "If it becomes a criminal case, women are more likely to be convicted, but female crime seldom becomes a criminal case", another respondent said. Yet another respondent pointed out that women often participate as facilitators, and also "understand what is going on", but are not necessarily convicted with the men involved. Even when both men and women are involved in financial crime, prosecutors may find it expedient to reduce the case so that men are prosecuted, while women are dismissed from the case. Sometimes, women are perceived as victims, even when they are active facilitators in the crime.

Table 4.4 Estimation based on gender of white-collar criminals

Approach 6: Gender of white-collar criminal

Category of white-collar crime victim	Figures from our database		Expert panel's estimate	
	Fraction of population (%)	Crime amount (million NOK)	Fraction convicted (%)	Sum of money (billion NOK)
Women	7.6	9.0	6.5	0.7
Men	92.4	20.4	10.5	11.5
Total	100			12.2

TOTAL CRIME MAGNITUDE

The final estimation technique in this research was to ask experts for their outright estimate of the total magnitude of white-collar crime in billions of NOK. The average response was 10.1 billion NOK.

Some of the respondents described their responses as "think of a number", and three experts declined to provide a number. However, most of the respondents both justified and reasoned their way to an answer, partly based on other estimates recorded for various types of economic crime. Two experts submitted answers that they directly connected to their previous percentage-based estimates. This worked fine for one of the experts, but not for the other one whose estimate of the money amount was far below what he had indicated for his conviction fraction.

During interviews, several respondents found it problematic to define limits for an estimate. For example, one expert—who incidentally had the highest estimate of the total magnitude of white-collar crime—said that he included "the organized part of social security fraud" in his estimate.

ALL APPROACHES COMBINED

Table 4.5 summarizes all seven approaches that resulted in an overall average of 11.9 billion NOK in white-collar crime damage annually in Norway. It varies from 10.1 billion NOK to 13.4 billion NOK.

Figure 4.2 visualizes the numbers in Table 4.5. The overall average of 11.9 billion NOK is illustrated by the last bar.

Table 4.5 Estimation based on seven approaches

All approaches combined	
Approach	Expert elicitation (billion NOK)
1	13.4
2	12.3
3	12.9
4	11.8
5	10.6
6	12.2
7	10.1
Average	**11.9**

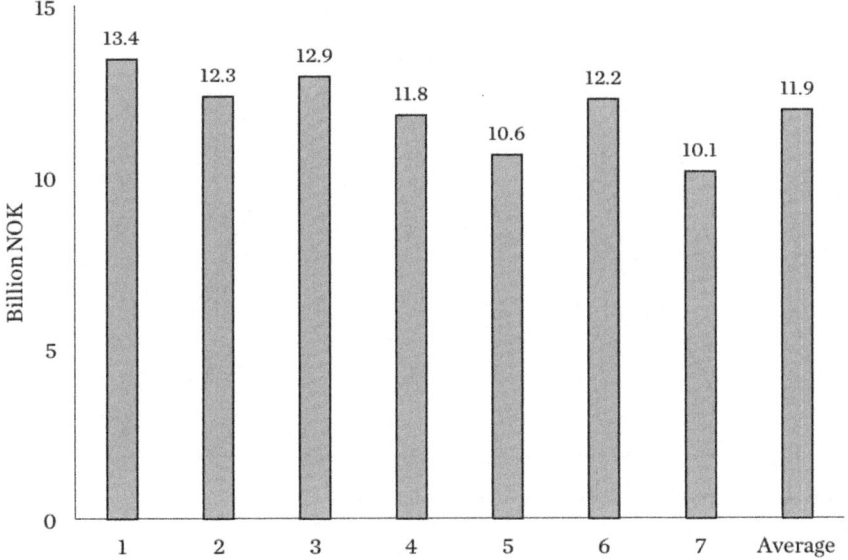

Fig. 4.2 Estimation of white-collar crime based on seven approaches

So far, we have presented research results in terms of average numbers for percentages, and millions and billions of NOK. Of course, there were substantial deviations in answers, both among experts and for each expert when indicating her or his own uncertainty. By combining our experts' probability distributions in approach 2 above, we are able to compute a probability distribution. Table 4.6 consists of four elements: (i) the visible

Table 4.6 Lower and upper bounds for the estimate of white-collar crime

Variation in estimates	
	White-collar crime (billion NOK)
Detected crime	1.1
Low estimate	4.4
Main estimate	11.9
High estimate	56.8

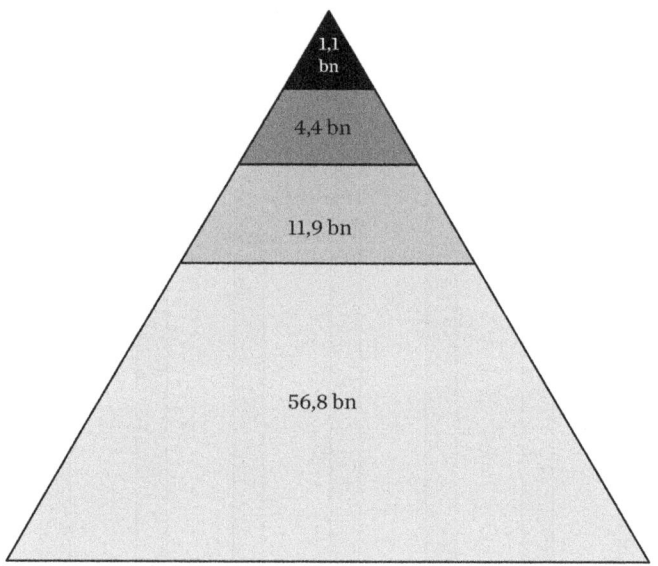

Fig. 4.3 Tip of the iceberg for white-collar crime

part of the iceberg, 1.1 billion NOK, (ii) the very optimistic low estimate of 4.4 billion NOK (less than 10 percent likely that the actual amount is lower, according to our experts), (iii) the most likely estimate of 11.9 billion NOK (the average estimate from our seven approaches), and (iv) the very pessimistic high estimate of 56.8 billion NOK (less than 10 percent likely that the actual amount is higher, according to our experts).

Figure 4.3 illustrates the uncertainty based on the numbers in Table 4.6. Later in the book we will compare these estimates to similar estimates made for social security fraud.

Our low estimate of 4.4 billion NOK per year roughly translates into three out of four white-collar criminals getting away every year. As we saw above, this equals Økokrim-boss Trond Eirik Schea's estimate from 2015. Our experts, however, claim that there is a 90 percent probability of this figure being too low, and that the problem we are facing is in fact larger.

Comparison with US Estimates

In comparison to the United States, 11.9 billion NOK is modest not only in comparison to the 40–80 billion NOK based on estimates from the US National White Collar Crime Center (also known as NW3C) (Huff et al. 2010), but also in comparison to the equivalent of 120 billion NOK suggested by the Association of Certified Fraud Examiners (ACFE 2008, 2014, 2016) published in 2016.

With a population of 5 million inhabitants in Norway as compared to the United States' 321 million inhabitants, the equivalent of $1.5 billion detected in Norway would be $96 billion in the United States. Ninety-six billion dollars is less than estimates from the Federal Bureau of Intelligence (FBI) and the Association of Certified Fraud Examiners, that approximate the annual cost of white-collar crime as being between $300 and $600 billion, according to NW3C (Huff et al. 2010).

NW3C estimates, in a report by Huff et al. (2010), the scope of white-collar crime in the United States at between 300 and 660 billion dollars. Given that the United States has a population of 321 million compared to 5 million in Norway, the equivalent range for Norway would be from 5 to 10 billion US dollars, if we assume that white-collar crime has the same prevalence in both nations. This interval in NOK is between 40 billion and 80 billion. Therefore, it is not inconceivable that our estimated amount (11.9 billion NOK) is conservative, and that the high estimate in Table 4.6 of 56.8 billion is not entirely unlikely.

In the United States, NW3C's mission is to provide a national support system for agencies involved in the prevention, investigation, and prosecution of economic crime and to support and partner with other appropriate entities in addressing security initiatives, as they relate to financial crime (www.nw3c.org).

REFERENCES

ACFE. (2008). *2008 Report to the Nation – On Occupational Fraud & Abuse*. Austin: Association of Certified Fraud Examiners.

ACFE. (2014). *Report to the Nations on Occupational Fraud and Abuse, 2014 Global Fraud Study*. Austin: Association of Certified Fraud Examiners.

ACFE. (2016). *CFE Code of Professional Standard*. Association of Certified Fraud Examiners. www.acfe.com/standards/

Huff, R., Desilets, K., & Kane, J. (2010). *The National Public Survey on White Cllar Crime*. Fairmont: National White Collar Crime Center. www.nw3c.org.

Open Access This chapter is licensed under the terms of the Creative Commons Attribution 4.0 International License (http://creativecommons.org/licenses/by/4.0/), which permits use, sharing, adaptation, distribution and reproduction in any medium or format, as long as you give appropriate credit to the original author(s) and the source, provide a link to the Creative Commons license and indicate if changes were made.

The images or other third party material in this chapter are included in the chapter's Creative Commons license, unless indicated otherwise in a credit line to the material. If material is not included in the chapter's Creative Commons license and your intended use is not permitted by statutory regulation or exceeds the permitted use, you will need to obtain permission directly from the copyright holder.

CHAPTER 5

Research Challenges

Abstract Expert elicitation is a research method designed to make estimations in areas where we have no certain knowledge. We tried to estimate the magnitude of white-collar crime in Norway. On our way to a final answer, we were faced with some obstacles in our research design. This chapter presents methodological challenges in estimating the magnitude of white-collar crime in a country in a year. The chapter makes a contribution to reflected learning from empirical research. The methodological issues are concerned with recruitment of experts, willingness and reactions from experts, and responses to different ways of representing the iceberg. A number of experts at first refused to participate. When they learned the identity of one of the researchers, this increased the response rate considerably.

Keywords Dealing with outliers • Distribution of experts • Median answers • Methodology • Meyer and Booker • Participation refusal • Recruitment of experts • Research design • Response confusion • Response rate

Expert elicitation is a research method designed to make estimations in areas where we have no knowledge, only indicators and experience. By systematically interviewing experts, we tried to estimate the magnitude of white-collar crime in Norway. On our way to a final answer, we were faced with obstacles in our research design. This chapter reports on our research journey by communicating our learning from methodological challenges when applying expert elicitation to estimate the size of an iceberg based on knowledge about the tip of the iceberg. In particular, participation refusals and response confusions are discussed.

This chapter presents methodological challenges when expert elicitation was applied to estimate the magnitude of white-collar crime in a country in a year. The chapter makes a contribution to reflected learning from empirical research. The methodological issues are concerned with the recruitment of experts, willingness and reactions from experts, and responses to different ways of representing the iceberg.

We were not completely successful in obtaining respondents as indicated in the previous chapter for several reasons. First, the category of victims was excluded, because victim experience is unfit for generalization. Next, some potential experts (e.g., executives at the stock exchange) refused to participate because of their role. Furthermore, several potential experts responded negatively to the email request. Our response rate was 33 percent. This is line with the literature, deeming a response rate of between one-third and three-querters as normal (Meyer and Booker 2001). A good distribution of experts rather than the participation rate among experts is regarded as more important in this kind of research.

Participation Refusal

A number of experts refused to participate in our interviews. It is interesting to study why they refused to contribute their expertise and what background they have.

1. Journalist: "I have nothing against contributing knowledge and experience on economic crime. And I think including the term 'white-collar crime' is a little old-fashioned today when the greatest threat to the Norwegian welfare state might be in complex, organized labor market crime, in an unattractive alliance between white-collar offenders and others. The classic white-collar offender is only one among many players in economic crime. But I do not want to guess percentages. I think it is not serious."

    This refusal is interesting from two perspectives. First, the journalist considers white-collar crime to be an old-fashioned term. We disagree, because ever since Sutherland (1939) coined this term, the criminal justice system as well as society has found it problematic to prosecute offenders in this category. This indicates that white-collar offences are still an unresolved issue in most countries. Next, the journalist does not want to guess percentages and thinks this method is not serious. We disagree again, as expert elicitation is a systematic approach beyond pure guesswork.

2. Victim: "My experience of such crime is more specific and related to one single case, and it gives me no foundation to consider the topic in general terms." Second victim (public sector manager): "We do not see it as appropriate to attend, but wish you good luck with [the] work and dedication in this field."

    This seems indeed to be a relevant objection to expert classification, since a victim typically has only one experience of white-collar crime. We know that generalizing from only one observation is not justifiable in research.

3. Bankruptcy auditor: "We have no case for refusal."
4. Internal auditor: "We have no case for refusal."
5. Tax administration employee: "We have no case for refusal."
6. Bank executive: "I do not have time, and I am generally unwilling to participate." Second bank executive: "I work in practice not with white-collar crime and am not qualified to answer the questions."

    Some organizations are very hierarchical, where executives are afraid of participating in external surveys. This might be the case for bank executives who are not at the top level in the organization. However, when the bank executives some days later were contacted by someone on the project team they know, and the person they know referred to previous contacts, then both bank executives changed their minds and agreed to participate. The first bank executive responded: "My initial answer was honest. We only deal with irregularities and misconduct among bank employees, and there are hardly any financial crime cases. I have not been able to build competence in this area. But nevertheless, I shall involve more experienced colleagues and answer questions to the best of my abilities." The second bank executive responded: "Since you are the one asking. OK."

7. External auditor: "I am on a mission abroad." Second external auditor: "I am basically happy [to be involved], but am completely snowed under until Christmas."

The first is an interesting excuse, since it is very often accepted that most busy people have more spare time while abroad than at home. Therefore, it is likely that the potential respondent found an excuse that he thought would be acceptable to the interviewer. The second external auditor is interesting as well, since it is workload that is communicated as the reason for not participating in the survey.

8. Police officer: "I am in a hurry and do not want to prioritize this."

Again, this is an interesting response, since police officers normally would like more attention directed at their work of combatting crime.

9. Stock exchange executive: "I thank you for asking, but do not want to participate in the survey."

We can only speculate on this refusal. One explanation might be that the stock exchange is sensitive to all kinds of issues and therefore members refrain from participation. Another reason might be that the Manifest Center for Social Analysis is considered a left-wing think tank so could be perceived negatively by a capitalist stock exchange.

10. Other: We have no case for refusal.

Meyer and Booker (2001) argue that it is important to recruit a wide range of experts. Maybe our range of experts could have been expanded to politicians who work in the criminal justice area, and whistleblowers who have reported white-collar offences, although they may have the same problem as victims, only one observation. A third group of experts might be attorneys who practice white-collar crime defense. A fourth group might be convicts, but again, they only know their own story, just like victims and whistleblowers. A fifth and most relevant group of experts is private investigators who conduct fraud examinations. Often, these financial crime specialists are former police detectives who have considerable experience in law enforcement, financial crime cases, and white-collar criminal behavior.

Furthermore, Meyer and Booker (2001) argue that persuading potential experts is not easy and should be handled with care. Perhaps we should not have started with an email from the Manifest Center for Social Analysis. Emails do not easily create a commitment, and Manifest is considered a left-wing think tank.

Manifest is in fact a known player in the Norwegian public arena with a clear affiliation not only to the social democratic but also to the socialist side of the community. Grassroots trade unions around the country appreciate the think tank, and they provide it with a lot of financial support.

Meyer and Booker (2001: 90) stress the importance of "motivating the experts through communication of intrinsic aspects of the project". In their experience, experts have responded well to these motivators: Recognition, experiencing something new and different, and need for meaning. Meyer and Booker (2001: 181) also stress common difficulties such as "experts resist the elicitation process or resist giving judgments under uncertainty".

Response Confusion

The first participant—an executive at the internal revenue service in Norway (Norwegian Tax Administration)—was faced with issues when she was asked to answer questions about both the total magnitude, as well as groups of the total, of white-collar crime occurrences. When she was asked about the total magnitude, she said that 5 percent of all white-collar crime is detected. However, when she was asked about groups, then most percentages were far above 5 percent, thus creating an average above 5 percent. For example, for groups of criminals, she estimated 15 percent, 30 percent and 4 percent. Similarly for categories of crime: Fraud 5 percent, theft 60 percent, manipulation 10 percent, and corruption 5 percent. The same occurred for groups of victims: Employers 20 percent, banks 10 percent, tax authority 10 percent, customers 5 percent, shareholders 40 percent, and others 5 percent. As a consequence, in subsequent interviews the interviewer needed to remind the respondent of the overall estimate when she was asked for subsequent estimates for groups of criminals, categories of crime, and groups of victims.

Maybe the interviewer's mistake was not related to what we asked experts to assess, but how we asked it. Kynn (2008) suggests that this aspect appears to have gone largely unnoticed by the statistical literature. The psychological aspects that are involved in eliciting probabilities have been largely ignored.

An interesting issue is whether or not—or to what extent—responding experts were able to keep track of their estimates during the interview. This issue can be exemplified by one of the experts who seemed to be on track during the interview by ending up with 14, 16, 11, 15 and 9 billion

NOK respectively. However, a surprise came at the end, when the expert was asked for the total magnitude of white-collar crime. The expert responded that to keep consistent with previous answers, the answer would be 3 billion NOK. From a methodological point of view this is fine, as there is no reason to argue that respondents should be able to keep track of previous estimates to keep consistency during the interview.

As illustrated by the two bank executives who first refused to participate, and then changed their minds as they were contacted by someone they knew on the project team, recruitment of experts can be influenced by previous relationships. The one researcher on the project team who they knew, is also quite well-known in Norway, because he frequently comments on white-collar crime cases in the media. This phenomenon caused even more experts to change their minds or to contribute the name of an alternative expert.

For example, one bankruptcy attorney responded:

> Nice to hear from you, and I hope we can have a chat over a coffee or lunch about your stay in the United States. I currently receive inquiries from both home and abroad to participate in various surveys and the like, and I have therefore set a limit to what I can participate in. I was not aware that the inquiry received regarding white-collar crime is something you are involved in. Of course I want to prioritize this and will set aside time for the interview.

Dealing with Outliers

As is to be expected in surveys like this, there was some variation in our experts' answers to the different questions. In line with the literature (Meyer and Booker 2001: 316), we were well aware of the danger of one single answer having a large influence on the average answer in small samples.

We considered using the median answer to all the questions as our estimate of the panel's joint assessment. However, a majority of our expert panel thought the share of white-collar criminals being caught and sentenced was well below the average answer, and only a few gave answers above the average. This means that our median answers would imply considerably higher crime amounts (20–25 percent) than the ones we present in the tables earlier. In our calculations, we chose to exclude both the highest and the lowest estimate given for each question. In the end, this led only to small adjustments relative to using the pure averages to calculate our results. This means that we implicitly chose to give the experts who claimed that a relatively high share of white-collar criminals were indeed caught, a higher weight in our calculations, than if we had used median values.

This chapter has described some obstacles and challenges in crime science. Specifically, it has addressed methodological challenges when attempting to determine the magnitude of white-collar crime based on expert elicitation. Recruitment of experts was indeed a challenge, and it seems that the two-stage approach of first email and then a phone interview is not very well suited to this exercise. Only when the identity of one of the well-known researchers became apparent to potential respondents, did the response rate increase considerably.

REFERENCES

Kynn, M. (2008). The 'Heuristics and Biases' Bias in Expert Elicitation. *Journal of the Royal Statistical Society, 171*, 239–264.

Meyer, M. A., & Booker, J. M. (2001). *Eliciting and Analyzing Expert Judgment: A Practical Guide, SIAM Books, ASA-SIAM Series on Statistics and Applied Probability*. Philadelphia: Society for Industrial and Applied Mathematics (SIAM).

Sutherland, E. H. (1939). White-Collar Criminality. *American Sociological Review, 5*, 1–12.

Open Access This chapter is licensed under the terms of the Creative Commons Attribution 4.0 International License (http://creativecommons.org/licenses/by/4.0/), which permits use, sharing, adaptation, distribution and reproduction in any medium or format, as long as you give appropriate credit to the original author(s) and the source, provide a link to the Creative Commons license and indicate if changes were made.

The images or other third party material in this chapter are included in the chapter's Creative Commons license, unless indicated otherwise in a credit line to the material. If material is not included in the chapter's Creative Commons license and your intended use is not permitted by statutory regulation or exceeds the permitted use, you will need to obtain permission directly from the copyright holder.

CHAPTER 6

More Research Results

Abstract We asked our experts what they think might be the reason for all those never caught or convicted: Is it because they are never detected, never investigated, never prosecuted, or because they are never convicted? All respondents agree that detection is the major reason for lack of law enforcement. Only 8 percent of white-collar criminals convicted to prison in Norway from 2009 to 2015 are women. On average, experts believe that 6.5 percent of all female offenders are caught, while 10.5 percent of all male offenders are caught. Experts confirm in this study that detection of white-collar crime is dependent on gender. Male criminals are detected more frequently than females. One explanation for this gender gap is the lack of suspicion towards female offenders.

Keywords Confirmation trap • Conviction • Criminal population size • Detection • Female offenders • Gender gap • Investigation • Pink-collar criminals • Prosecution • Variation in responses

In a previous chapter, we applied expert elicitation to estimate the amount of money lost from white-collar crime every year in Norway. The panel of experts was asked to estimate the magnitude of white-collar crime as well as reasons for the lack of convictions.

The visible tip represents around 10 percent of the total iceberg, as suggested by our experts.

© The Author(s) 2018
P. Gottschalk, L. Gunnesdal, *White-Collar Crime in the Shadow Economy*,
https://doi.org/10.1007/978-3-319-75292-1_6

We asked all our experts for an opinion on why people are not caught or convicted: Is it because they are never detected? Is it because they are never investigated? Is it because they are never prosecuted? Is it because they are never convicted?

Lack of Detection and Conviction

We asked respondents to distribute the remaining percentages from 100 percent after subtracting 9.4 percent for those caught and convicted. The average response from 15 experts is as follows:

- *Lack of detection: 59 percent.* For example, it may be easy to commit financial crime and to hide illicit transactions among legal transactions. There may also be a consensus culture at board level whereby management is not being asked critical questions and is thus avoiding transparency and control. One respondent said: "The police always complain that they are lacking resources, but I also think that detectives are not good enough." Another respondent pointed out that there are "powerful forces that prevent people from whistleblowing".
- *Lack of investigation: 19 percent.* The police do not have the capacity and must therefore dismiss criminal cases. One respondent pointed out that although lack of detection is a problem, she had noted that the police dismiss many cases. Nineteen percent of all white-collar criminals are assumed to be detected, but not investigated, although they are guilty.
- *Lack of prosecution: 8 percent.* The police do not have competence and are therefore not successful in obtaining evidence sufficient to get likely convictions. Eight percent of all white-collar criminals are assumed to be detected and investigated, but not prosecuted, although they are guilty.
- *Lack of conviction: 5 percent.* Defense attorneys are often successful in their substance, defense, symbolic defense, and information control. Prosecutors tend to be legal generalists, while defense attorneys tend to be white-collar crime specialists. Judges in court are afraid of miscarriages of justice, so prefer to acquit a guilty person rather than convict a possibly innocent person. Five percent of all white-collar criminals are assumed to be detected, investigated and prosecuted, but not sentenced, although they are guilty.

It is interesting to note that all respondents agree that detection is the major reason for the lack of law enforcement. While their estimates vary, lack of detection is the main reason for all respondents, varying from 40 percent to 90 percent with an average of 59 percent. The expert with the highest estimate is an internal revenue executive at the Norwegian Tax Administration, while the expert with the lowest estimate is an investment banker. This implies that the investment banker believes in a much higher detection rate for white-collar criminals, which is indeed the case given the investment banker's response to the first question.

Given that 59 percent of all white-collar criminals are never detected, a challenging responsibility rests with professionals who are supposed to detect financial crime. These professionals include internal and external auditors, compliance officers, audit committees, and management at all levels.

When offenders are detected, they may nevertheless not be investigated. The fraction not investigated varies from 3 percent to 30 percent. The bankruptcy auditor is the one who believes that many detected criminal cases are never investigated, indicating that almost one-third of all white-collar criminals belong in this category. The bank executive shares this opinion. The average response is 19 percent in this category, which is surprisingly high, indicating that experts think that the police are often reluctant to look into white-collar crime cases.

When offenders are detected and then investigated, they may nevertheless not be prosecuted. They are assumed to be guilty, but prosecutors decide not to bring them to court as defendants, maybe because of lack of evidence. Experts estimate this population fraction to range from 1 percent to 20 percent. It is the private investigator who believes in a figure of 20 percent, while it is the internal revenue executive who believes in only 1 percent. The average is 8 percent.

When offenders are guilty and defending themselves in court, they may nevertheless not be convicted. Experts estimate this population fraction to range from 1 percent to 10 percent. Again, the private investigator believes in the highest fraction, this time of guilty criminals whose cases are dismissed. And again, it is the internal revenue executive who believes in the lowest fraction (i.e., this expert believes that almost all guilty defendants in court are sentenced). The average is 5 percent.

Example: An Investigative Journalist

To illustrate the variation in responses to our seven expert elicitation approaches, we select an investigative journalist, since investigative journalists are credited with the most detections of white-collar crime. Table 6.1 shows the journalist's estimates resulting from the seven approaches.

It is interesting to note that while this expert suggests a fraction of 8 percent, all levels of offenders have a higher detection rate—according to the expert—as illustrated in approach 3. Furthermore, this expert disagrees with other experts, as he believes that the detection rate for male and female offenders is the same.

Table 6.1 Seven different expert estimations of the magnitude of white-collar crime

#	Estimation technique for the magnitude of white-collar crime	Fraction of offender population caught and convicted (%)	Magnitude of white-collar crime (billion NOK)
1	Fraction of total	8	**14.2**
2	Fraction, probability distribution	10	**11.0**
3	• Level 1	13	4.4
	• Level 2	23	2.0
	• Level 3	30	0.5
	Groups of offenders		**6.9**
4	• Fraud	15	4.2
	• Theft	5	0.2
	• Manipulation	5	9.4
	• Corruption	5	0.5
	Groups of offences		**14.3**
5	• Employer	20	0.7
	• Tax	20	2.0
	• Bank	5	4.9
	• Customer	10	1.7
	• Shareholder	5	2.6
	• Other	15	0.3
	Groups of victims		**12.2**
6	• Female	8	0.5
	• Male	8	13.7
	Gender		**14.2**
7	Estimate of total amount		**10.0**
	Average magnitude		**11.8**

CRIMINAL POPULATION SIZE

About 58 white-collar criminals are convicted to prison every year in Norway. We assume this is 9.4 percent of the total criminal population. Thus, the total population is estimated at 617 offenders per year who commit financial crime that year.

The estimation of total population size for various phenomena of crime is an important factor that is critical for criminal justice policy and priorities in law enforcement. Rossmo and Routledge (1990) discuss methods for estimating the size of a criminal population from police records. This is similar to our estimation based on convicted white-collar criminals. In their research, they found that police records are virtually unaffected by a potentially large pool of criminals as they tried to predict the size of population for migrating (or fleeing) fugitives and for street prostitutes.

GENDER PERSPECTIVES ON CRIME

Only 8 percent of white-collar criminals imprisoned in Norway from 2009 to 2015 are women. Ninety-two percent are men. In a number of research articles, it has been speculated why the female fraction is so low. Interestingly, our experts unknowingly indicated a similarly low female fraction by providing an average estimate of 6.5 percent female detection rate.

In terms of gender, experts responded as follows:

1. An investigative journalist stated that 8 percent of female offenders and 8 percent of male offenders are detected—thus implying no gender gap.
2. A bankruptcy attorney stated that 5 percent of female offenders and 3 percent of male offenders are detected—thus a gender gap favoring the detection of women.
3. An internal auditor stated that 2 percent of female offenders and 7 percent of male offenders are detected—thus a gender gap favoring the detection of men.
4. A tax clerk in the internal revenue service stated that 5 percent of female offenders and 20 percent of male offenders are detected—thus a gender gap favoring the detection of men.
5. A tax clerk in the internal revenue service stated that 5 percent of female offenders and 5 percent of male offenders are detected—thus implying no gender gap.

6. A tax clerk in the internal revenue service stated that 3 percent of female offenders and 7 percent of male offenders are detected—thus a gender gap favoring the detection of men.
7. A bank manager stated that 10 percent of female offenders and 10 percent of male offenders are detected—thus implying no gender gap.
8. A bank manager stated that 3 percent of female offenders and 3 percent of male offenders are detected—thus implying no gender gap.
9. A police investigator stated that 10 percent of female offenders and 25 percent of male offenders are detected—thus a gender gap favoring the detection of men.
10. A corruption researcher stated that 3 percent of female offenders and 8 percent of male offenders are detected—thus a gender gap favoring the detection of men.
11. A private investigator stated that 15 percent of female offenders and 23 percent of male offenders are detected—thus a gender gap favoring the detection of men.
12. A private investigator stated that 5 percent of female offenders and 4 percent of male offenders are detected—thus a gender gap favoring the detection of women.
13. A corporate investor meant that 30 percent of female offenders and 30 percent of male offenders are detected—thus implying no gender gap.
14. A defense attorney stated that 10 percent of female offenders and 10 percent of male offenders are detected—thus implying no gender gap.
15. A social security manager stated that 1 percent of female offenders and 5 percent of male offenders are detected—thus a gender gap favoring the detection of men.

The panel of experts provides no coherent response. Rather, experts disagree both in terms of percentages and in terms of relative percentages. Out of 15 experts, six believe there is no gender gap, two believe that more women than men are detected, while seven believe that more men than women are detected. The last result seems to be a common view among both researchers and practitioners, as discussed in the literature.

On average, experts believe that 6.5 percent of all female offenders are caught, while 10.5 percent of all male offenders are caught. Again, this is in line with common understanding. We know that 8 percent of all convicted white-collar (pink-collar) criminals in Norway are women. If we assume that their relative detection rate is only a fraction of the male detection rate (6.5/10.5) then we can assume that the real female offender fraction in the iceberg is around 12 percent. This means that experts suggest a 12 percent fraction of female white-collar criminals in Norway rather than the 8 percent fraction of female offenders detected.

This section is not concerned with the general gender gap as such in white-collar crime, where women commit less white-collar crime compared to men. Reasons for the general gender gap include lack of opportunity, lack of motive, and lack of rationalization (Holtfreter 2015; Steffensmeier et al. 2013).

Rather, this section is concerned with the lack of detection of female white-collar criminals. The relative lack of detection can be explained by several factors. First, women are to a lesser extent suspected of financial crime. The environment is generally less suspicious of women than of men, and tends to decriminalize women. To the extent a crime is detected, a woman is not considered or treated as the main suspect. She is either treated as a criminal follower or as a criminal victim in a typical criminal investigation when there are more people involved in the crime. Detection risk is linked to general reasons why women to a far lesser extent than men are convicted of white-collar crime, namely that women generally are not convicted of crime when compared to men.

A simple experiment we have often performed with different audiences is based on the question: Who would you bribe? You would like to build a new home on a property that is designated for public recreation. You have the choice of bribing a female or male official in the municipality. Considering all the audiences over the years, a large majority vote almost exclusively to choose men. Almost no one would bribe a female official. There are two learning points here. First, very few people think that a woman is corrupt, thereby reducing the detection rate. Second, because almost no one would bribe a woman, then a woman has less opportunity to be a criminal.

Possibly women are smarter criminals than men. Again, when an experiment is carried out with an audience, most agree with this statement. One reason for relative smartness is that women may tend to stop criminal activities before it is too late. They are considered smart and manipulative and often get their way using indirect means. Women are usually brought up and thought of as the weaker sex in society and thus have to resort to other ways to accomplish things. It may seem that they only do work and carry out tasks that are important for the company to get done, while men only do what they would like to do. Women monopolize areas in which they seem innocent, such as care, health, and environment. Women tend to talk most passionately about ethics, morals, and social responsibility, so it is almost impossible for others to think that they are criminals. Thus, the detection fraction for women will be lower than for men. The fact that women talk most often about ethics is confirmed by a study carried out by Dodge (2009). She refers to her Canadian study in which 94 percent of all companies with an executive board with three or more female members had established guidelines for conflicts of interest. Studies such as this can help confirm that women, to a greater extent than men, are concerned that their company should follow rules and policy lines to develop and maintain a good reputation.

Some researchers make the distinction between ethics and being ethical. Research by O'Fallon and Butterfield (2005) shows no difference between women and men when it comes to making ethical and unethical decisions. Dollar et al. (2001) found, nevertheless, that a greater fraction of women in parliament is associated with a lower extent of corruption. But here, detection rate can play a role. Research findings that women are more preoccupied with ethics and demonstrate stronger ethical attitudes than men is confirmed in earlier studies as well.

Lower relative detection rate can also be explained by the tendency that white-collar crime only captures financial crime of a large magnitude. This leads to a smaller female detection fraction because the average monetary amount in female crime tends to be lower than the average amount in male crime. In addition, women may be cleverer in staying below the radar and avoiding attention by keeping quiet and stopping criminal activities at an earlier stage. A relatively low detection rate might also be explained because investigators and detectives misunderstand female roles in crime and tend to perceive women as victims of crime. Women typically present themselves as victims by claiming to be coerced by men.

On the other hand, men have a reputation of being the gender that takes initiatives at high risk and, therefore, they are more easily detected. They are also detected because they like to show off their material success. The police also contribute to the low detection fraction for white-collar female criminals compared with other kinds of crime. When the police attend a family because of a domestic crisis, the main suspect is almost always the man, and the man is typically removed from the situation. Likewise, if the police find incriminating documents in the home, it is assumed that they belong to the man.

From a historical perspective, society has accepted a gender culture in which it is more usual for men to be criminals. This can be explained by the confirmation trap, in which humans tend to try to confirm what they already think they know. When there are so few convicted women, then there must be fewer female criminals. When there are fewer female criminals, the police will pursue male criminals. When female criminals are not pursued, then fewer women will be convicted.

Yet another reason for a relatively lower detection fraction is that organizations internally treat suspicion as well as detection differently for men and women. Maybe it is because it is more usual for the board, management, and auditors to hand cases of male misconduct and crime over to the police. One might be more cautious and afraid of taking the wrong steps in terms of discrimination by accusing female employees of crime. It can be very convenient to forget about female misconduct and concentrate on male misconduct in internal investigations. Finally, it can be argued that traditional investigations are more suited to male suspects than to female suspects.

While some women may stop in time and not be detected, men typically have a longer criminal career than women. However, it is not easy to tell exactly when a criminal career should be described as finished or terminated, and there is little evidence in the literature. It has been suggested that women's average criminal careers last just under five years, and men's more than seven years.

In conclusion, experts confirm in this study that detection of white-collar crime is dependent on gender. Male criminals are detected more frequently than females. One explanation for this gender gap is the lack of suspicion towards female offenders. Women are often considered more ethical. In organizations, one might be more cautious and afraid of taking the wrong steps in terms of discrimination by accusing female employees of crime. It can also be very convenient to forget about female misconduct and concentrate on male misconduct in internal investigations. Finally, it can be argued that traditional investigations are more suited to male suspects than to female suspects.

REFERENCES

Dodge, M. (2009). *Women and White Collar Crime*. New York: Prentice Hall.
Dollar, D., Fisman, R., & Gatti, R. (2001). Are Women Really the "Fairer" Sex? Corruption and Women in Government. *Journal of Economic Behavior & Organization, 46*(4), 423–429.
Holtfreter, K. (2015). General Theory, Gender-Specific Theory, and White-Collar Crime. *Journal of Financial Crime, 22*(4), 422–431.
O'Fallon, M., & Butterfield, K. D. (2005). A Review of the Empirical Ethical Decision-Making Literature: 1996–2003. *Journal of Business Ethics, 59*(4), 375–413.
Rossmo, D. K., & Routledge, R. (1990). Estimating the Size of Criminal Populations. *Journal of Quantitative Criminology, 6*(3), 293–314.
Steffensmeier, D., Schwartz, J., & Roche, M. (2013). Gender and Twenty-First-Century Corporate Crime: Female Involvement and the Gender Gap in Enron-Era Corporate Frauds. *American Sociological Review, 5*, 1–12.

Open Access This chapter is licensed under the terms of the Creative Commons Attribution 4.0 International License (http://creativecommons.org/licenses/by/4.0/), which permits use, sharing, adaptation, distribution and reproduction in any medium or format, as long as you give appropriate credit to the original author(s) and the source, provide a link to the Creative Commons license and indicate if changes were made.

The images or other third party material in this chapter are included in the chapter's Creative Commons license, unless indicated otherwise in a credit line to the material. If material is not included in the chapter's Creative Commons license and your intended use is not permitted by statutory regulation or exceeds the permitted use, you will need to obtain permission directly from the copyright holder.

CHAPTER 7

Student Elicitation for Estimation

Abstract A class of bachelor-level students, who were attending lectures in a course on financial crime at the business school in Oslo in the spring term 2017, was asked to fill in a questionnaire with most of the questions we asked our expert panel. When these answers are compared to the expert elicitation earlier in the book, we find that students believe in a slightly higher conviction rate among all those who commit white-collar crime. Our experts believed it was 9.4 percent, while students believe it is 13.5 percent. Rather than focusing on the difference between these estimates, it makes sense to claim that they are similar. Both experts and students believe that the iceberg is many times bigger than what is visible above the surface.

Keywords Comparison • Conviction rate • Corruption Detection • Fraud • Gender ratio • Manipulation • Offender groups • Student elicitation • Theft • Victim groups

A class of bachelor-level students, who were attending lectures in an elective course on financial crime at the business school in Oslo in the spring term of 2017, were asked to fill in a questionnaire. The questionnaire had statements derived from the expert elicitation in terms of estimates to calculate the magnitude of white-collar crime.

Fraction of White-Collar Criminals

We asked students the following question: How large a fraction of all white-collar criminals that commit financial crime in this country do you think is detected and imprisoned? The average answer from the experts was 9.4 percent, or that about one out of ten criminals are caught and sentenced. Students believed slightly more offenders are caught and brought to justice. Their average response was 13.5 percent, which means that they think one out of seven white-collar criminals are caught and sentenced. Their response results in an estimate of 9.3 billion NOK.

Fraction with Probability Distribution

This was not part of the student survey.

Fraction of Offender Groups

Three levels of offenders were defined in this research: (i) top level offenders such as executives and attorneys, (ii) middle level offenders such as investors and accounting managers, and (iii) basic level offenders such as accounting clerks and carpenters. As listed in Table 7.1, respondents believe the fraction of convictions is slightly lower among top level offenders. This approach resulted in an estimate of white-collar crime of the magnitude of 10 billion NOK.

Table 7.1 Estimation based on levels of white-collar criminals

Approach 3: Type of white-collar offender

Level of white-collar criminals	Figures from our database		Student's estimate	
	Fraction of population (%)	Crime amount (million NOK)	Fraction convicted (%)	Sum of money (billion NOK)
Top level	28.4	33.0	12.5	4.8
Middle level	46.1	16.6	12.7	3.9
Basic level	25.5	9.7	13.2	1.3
Total	100			10.0

Fraction of Crime Categories

Distinction is made between fraud, theft, manipulation, and corruption. As listed in Table 7.2, students believe theft is most often detected and convicted. Students believe manipulation is most seldom convicted, while experts believe that corruption most seldom leads to conviction. This is an interesting response difference; students may think that manipulation is associated with being smart. This approach resulted in an estimate of white-collar crime of the magnitude of 8.6 billion NOK.

Fraction of Victim Groups

Distinction is made between the following groups of victims: employers, banks, the tax service, customers, shareholders, and others. As listed in Table 7.3, students believe bank fraud, tax evasion, and insider trading

Table 7.2   Estimation based on categories of white-collar crime

Approach 4: Type of white-collar crime

	Figures from our database		Student's estimate	
Category of white-collar crime	Fraction of population (%)	Crime amount (million NOK)	Fraction convicted (%)	Sum of money (billion NOK)
Fraud	42.6	25.4	15.8	4.4
Theft	4.2	4.8	17.0	0.1
Manipulation	35.3	22.8	13.2	3.9
Corruption	17.9	2.5	16.9	0.2
Total	100			8.6

Table 7.3   Estimation based on categories of white-collar crime victims

Approach 5: Type of victim

	Figures from our database		Student's estimate	
Category of white-collar crime victim	Fraction of population (%)	Crime amount (million NOK)	Fraction convicted (%)	Sum of money (billion NOK)
Employer	27.9	8.7	14.8	1.1
Banks	14.2	49.5	17.2	2.6
Tax authority	22.1	18.0	16.2	1.7
Customers	16.4	17.3	14.3	1.3
Shareholders	7.4	29.8	15.2	0.9
Others	12.0	6.9	13.5	0.4
Total	100			8.0

achieves a higher conviction rate than employer fraud, customer fraud, and cases involving other victims. Both banks and tax authorities have their own criminal investigation units that are able to provide sufficient evidence so that prosecutors are often able to achieve convictions in court. This approach resulted in an estimate of white-collar crime of the magnitude of 8.0 billion NOK.

Gender Fractions

Only 7.6 percent of convicted white-collar criminals in Norway are women, while 92.4 percent are men. The rate of detection and conviction may be dependent on gender. Our student respondents think so, as shown in Table 7.4, where respondents believe that only 8.7 percent of female white-collar criminals are caught and brought to justice, while 18.7 percent of male white-collar criminals are convicted. The gender ratio is thus 2.15 in terms of detection (dividing 18.7 by 8.7). When we multiply female convicts by the gender ratio, it results in a predicted female fraction of white-collar criminals of 15 percent and a male fraction of 85 percent rather than 7.6 percent and 92.4 percent respectively. This approach resulted in an estimate of white-collar crime of the magnitude of 7.0 billion NOK.

Total Crime Magnitude

The final estimation technique in this research was to ask the students about a value for the total magnitude of white-collar crime in billions of NOK. The average response was 90.7 billion NOK. Obviously, bachelor-

Table 7.4 Estimation based on gender of white-collar criminals

Approach 6: Gender of white-collar criminal

	Figures from our database		Student's estimate	
Category of white-collar crime victim	Fraction of population (%)	Crime amount (million NOK)	Fraction convicted (%)	Sum of money (billion NOK)
Women	7.6	9.0	8.7	0.5
Men	92.4	20.4	18.7	6.5
Total	100			7.0

level students, most aged 22, have problems with large money values. Some even suggested several hundred billion NOK.

Table 7.5 summarizes all the relevant approaches that resulted in an overall average of 8.5 billion NOK attributed to white-collar criminal damage annually in Norway. Approach 2 was not applied in the student survey, and approach 7 (estimating money values in billions of NOK) resulted in a totally confusing average, and was thus left out.

When this student survey is compared to the expert elicitation earlier in the book, we find that students believe in a slightly higher conviction rate among all those who commit white-collar crime. Likewise, experts believed in an overall average value of 11.9 billion NOK, while the students' value was 8.5 billion NOK. Rather than focusing on the difference between these two estimates, it probably makes more sense to claim that they are similar. Both experts and students believe that the iceberg is many times bigger than what is visible on the surface.

The final question to students in the questionnaire was about their own knowledge: How do you judge your own knowledge of white-collar crime on a scale from 1 (little knowledge) to 10 (a lot of knowledge)? The average response was 4.76 with standard deviation of 1.335.

Depending on the self-reported knowledge level, it is interesting to study whether there is a significant correlation with the estimated percentages in the above approaches. Statistical analysis reveals that knowledge level is only related to middle level offenders, where respondents who report a higher knowledge level believe in a lower conviction rate for middle level white-collar criminals.

Table 7.5 Student's estimation based on five approaches

All approaches combined	
Approach	Student's estimate (billion NOK)
1	9.3
2	–
3	10.0
4	8.6
5	8.0
6	7.0
7	(90.7)
Average	8.5

Expert–Student Comparison

Why is the iceberg eight or ten times greater than what is visible in Norwegian courts? Why are most white-collar criminals in Norway never convicted? While experts suggest that the main reason is lack of detection, students suggest that the main reason is lack of investigation, as illustrated in Table 7.6.

Table 7.6 Distribution of iceberg elements for white-collar crime

	Experts (%)	Students (%)
Lack of detection	59	15
Lack of investigation	19	29
Lack of prosecution	8	24
Lack of conviction	5	19
Convictions	9	13
Total	100	100

Open Access This chapter is licensed under the terms of the Creative Commons Attribution 4.0 International License (http://creativecommons.org/licenses/by/4.0/), which permits use, sharing, adaptation, distribution and reproduction in any medium or format, as long as you give appropriate credit to the original author(s) and the source, provide a link to the Creative Commons license and indicate if changes were made.

The images or other third party material in this chapter are included in the chapter's Creative Commons license, unless indicated otherwise in a credit line to the material. If material is not included in the chapter's Creative Commons license and your intended use is not permitted by statutory regulation or exceeds the permitted use, you will need to obtain permission directly from the copyright holder.

CHAPTER 8

Social Security Fraud

Abstract Social security fraud and white-collar offences represent serious forms of financial crime. We compare previous estimates of social security fraud in Norway made using a comparable methodology to that which we have applied to white-collar crime. Although the estimated 9.8 billion NOK for social security fraud is enormous in a nation like Norway, we suggest that the amount for white-collar crime is even bigger. We also apply social conflict theory to discuss the issue of priorities in law enforcement between social security fraud versus white-collar crime. According to social conflict theory, the justice system is biased and designed to protect the wealthy and powerful. They will never accept the view that minor fraud prosecution represents a kind of over-criminalization targeted at the losers in society.

Keywords Benefits • Detection • Estimated magnitude • Expert elicitation • Fraud • NAV • Norway • Police priorities • Social conflict theory • Social security

Both social security fraud and white-collar offenses represent serious forms of financial crime causing harm and victims in society. The police have limited resources to investigate economic crime and have to prioritize their resources by dropping a large portion of cases (Brooks and Button 2011). The question we ask here is: Should law enforcement primarily dismiss social security fraud cases or white-collar crime cases?

The two types of cases are in many ways two extremes on the scale of economic criminals. While social security fraud is committed by people who basically need financial help from the community to live decent lives, white-collar crime is committed by individuals in the upper-echelons of society who abuse their positions to enrich themselves or the organizations they are associated with.

In this chapter, we compare previous estimates of social security fraud in Norway, made using a comparable methodology to that which we have applied to white-collar crime in this book. We also apply social conflict theory to discuss the issue of priorities in law enforcement between social security fraud versus white-collar crime.

A number of situations are viewed as social security fraud, including misuse of benefits, making false statements on claims, and buying or selling social security cards. Concealing information that affects eligibility for benefits is also considered to be fraud.

People who represent social security recipients commit fraud if they misuse the benefits they are entrusted with (Lensvelt-Mulders et al. 2006). It is considered fraud when people knowingly provide inaccurate information when they apply for social security benefits. Anyone receiving social security disability benefits must inform the social security administration if they also receive workers' compensation benefits from their organizations where they are or were employed.

A Social Security Fraudster

She is 73 years old and was sentenced to prison for 18 months by the Agder court of appeal (upholding the decision of a lower court) in Norway in 2015. She had been paid a disability pension of just under 1 million NOK over five and a half years, without disclosing that she once had revenues from fortune telling totaling 1.7 million NOK ($212,000). Her income as a fortune teller was not reported to the authorities.

She worked as a fortune teller in a business that provided fortune telling by phone. The fortune telling service was marketed in newspapers and magazines. Each fortune teller had a unique artist name and a dedicated phone number. Callers were charged by elapsed time and paid in most cases over the phone. The minute price was 7 NOK (88 cents).

When she started to work as a fortune teller, she contacted her local social security office and asked what she was allowed to earn in addition to her disability pension. She was told that she could make no more than

5,000 NOK ($625) per month. She followed instructions received from NAV (the Norwegian labor and welfare administration/Norwegian social security authority), and she was paid 5,000 NOK per month for about ten months per year from startup until she went over the retirement age after six years. The sum of 5,000 NOK was paid to her regardless of how much she actually worked as a fortune teller. She did not work very much, partly because she had to care for her elderly mother for a long time. After retirement, she has legally worked and earned by the hour. Her salary has been taxed in the normal way. She denies receiving any funds beyond the specified amount of 5,000 NOK per month.

The Agder (2015) court of appeal, however, found beyond any reasonable and sensible doubt that she had received remuneration for her fortune telling business beyond the 5,000 NOK that were reported to the tax authorities and NAV. The court of appeal disregarded the possibility that other people may have used the same phone number, or that there has been a confusion between different fortune tellers.

The court of appeal found it proven that for many years she had conducted a fortune telling service that was paid for in cash from the business, which is why it was not registered in bank transfers or bank deposits.

She told the court that she has lived very soberly, that she had taken only one holiday trip in 23 years, and that she has an old car bought with borrowed money. She told the court that she has borrowed money from the bank for the renovation and repair of her residential property, that she has an open and straightforward relationship with the bank, and that she has communicated with NAV on the topic of income for work in addition to her disability pension.

The Larvik district court sentenced her to imprisonment for 18 months. The judge wrote in the verdict:

> As a general rule, the sentencing court emphasizes the need for deterrent mechanisms regarding social security fraud and tax evasion. On social security fraud, which is the most serious offence by the defendant, the Supreme Court has emphasized that such cases involve abuse of key welfare benefits that largely is based on confidence that recipients provide an honest and correct description of their economic and social situation. For many, the barrier against committing this kind of crime is low, since it is society at large and not individuals who is victim of the crime. It is therefore essential that this type of violations is met with a tactile reaction. This is particularly true in the case of fraud in the magnitude that we are facing here.

The court of appeal endorsed the district court's standpoint. The court of appeal referred to a number of previous convictions for social security fraud, where offenders were sentenced to ten months' imprisonment for a fraud of 650,000 NOK, one year for a fraud of 1.1 million NOK, 16 months for a fraud of 1 million NOK, and 18 months for a fraud of 2 million NOK.

The court of appeal wrote that "even if the defendant has experienced many dramatic and sad events in her immediate surroundings over the years, the court does not find any grounds to argue that there are mitigating circumstances in this case".

A claim of 993,994 NOK was submitted by NAV for payment of compensation. This claim was upheld, and she was ordered to pay this amount to NAV.

Different Kinds of Icebergs

Estimating the magnitude of white-collar crime is arguably a greater challenge than estimating social security fraud or tax evasion, as illustrated in Fig. 8.1. The only known indication of its scope is the total number of convicted white-collar criminals. As illustrated in the figure, this is a small circle within the larger circle of total white-collar crime. When estimating social security fraud or tax evasion, there are two known amounts, not just one: the detected fraud as well as the total social security payments made, and the detected evasion as well as the total tax revenue owing.

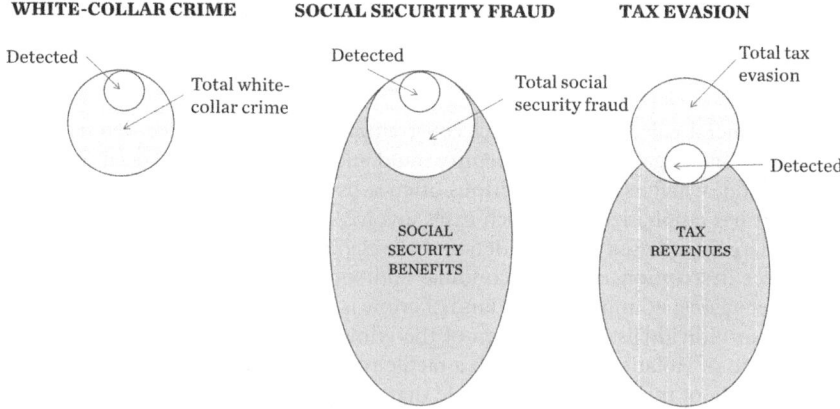

Fig. 8.1 Estimation of the magnitude of different forms of financial crime

In estimating probabilities, both psychology and statistics are needed to guide expert elicitation. When experts are asked about the magnitude of the three different kinds of economic crime illustrated in the figure, psychological biases may, for example, cause left-wing respondents to claim a large fraction of undetected white-collar crime, while right-wing respondents may claim a large fraction of undetected social security fraud, simply because they disagree about law enforcement priorities. Kynn (2008) argues that humans make probability judgments through a series of heuristics which lead to systematic and predictable biases. She suggests that researchers should be equally concerned with what they ask experts to assess and how they ask it. Probability elicitation is influenced by a number of factors such as the tendency to judge the frequency of an event by the ease of remembering specific examples. Furthermore, anchoring and adjustment is the tendency to anchor a probability estimate at an initial value and then to adjust it outwards. Insufficient adjustment results in biases of overestimation or underestimation when judging.

As we shall see below, the Norwegian government paid 194 billion NOK in social security, including public pensions to the elderly, to inhabitants in Norway in 2015 (the dark gray area in the figure). It is claimed that 9.8 billion NOK should not have been paid out, and the government prosecutes recipients for wrongful payments. The estimated fraction of social security fraud is thus 5 percent (the light gray area).

When estimating the magnitude of white-collar crime, we were faced with the opposite situation. We knew the fraction amount, but not the total amount. We knew that people were convicted of a total of 1.1 billion NOK annually in white-collar crime cases. Our experts suggest that this is only 10 percent of the total.

The magnitude of white-collar crime is affected by a number of factors. Three main effects are as follows:

1. The gain that can be achieved serves to avoid a threat or to safeguard a possibility. For example, a more ambitious goal orientation leads to a stronger desire for profit. This is the economic dimension of convenience theory.
2. The effort required to commit financial crime, the risk that the offense is detected, as well as encouragement from others to break the law. For example, a chief executive may act alone without anyone noticing or controlling him or her. This is the organizational dimension of convenience theory.

3. Excuses that can justify the offense by lack of self-control and application of neutralization techniques. For example, the offender may argue that everyone else does it, and that there is something wrong with the law. This is the behavioral dimension of convenience theory.

The magnitude of social security fraud is affected by a number of factors, such as:

- The effort required to commit fraud. The effort may vary depending on whether it is an active or a passive act, where the offender supplies misleading information or simply does not supply sufficient information.
- The risk of detection of the crime. Most important is the subjective detection probability, which is the likelihood, as perceived by the offender, of getting caught and being brought to justice.
- The gain that can be achieved in the fraud, and the importance of that gain for the offender.
- Encouragement from others to commit the crime. For example, a network of social security abusers invites newcomers into a fraud scheme.
- Excuses that can justify the offense to the offender. For example, even if social security payments are quite reasonable in Norway, recipients of social support certainly do not belong to the wealthy part of the population. An offender may feel entitled to extra profit.

MAGNITUDE OF SOCIAL SECURITY FRAUD

At least in Norway, and probably in many other countries as well, law enforcement has a tendency to focus on losers in society who commit crimes. Sutherland (1939), who coined the term "white-collar crime", was the first to point out that the elite in society is seldom prosecuted when it members break the laws developed by the elite. Although this factor was identified decades ago, many nations, such as Norway, still struggle to fight financial crime committed by members of the upper class in society. When cases come up, then they are often treated as single cases of individuals who were unfortunate in their positions. Against this background, it is interesting to compare the estimated magnitude of social security fraud with the estimated magnitude of white-collar crime.

In recent years, the Norwegian media have repeatedly directed much attention towards social security fraud. There are stories of the Norwegian social security authority (NAV) reporting not just hundreds, but over the years thousands, of people for fraud to the police. The secretary for labor in the Norwegian government repeatedly says she will make NAV swindlers unsafe. NAV is able to provide solid evidence that fraudulent recipients have received too much support from the social security system, and via the police such swindlers are prosecuted in the courts where some are convicted and sentenced to imprisonment.

In its report from 2011, the Norwegian analysis bureau Proba (2011) concludes regarding sick pay that at least 6 percent of payments are probably wrongly paid to beneficiaries who deliberately misinform NAV. This estimate emerged from questioning a group of experts, consisting of scientists, medical doctors, and mainly employees at NAV.

In a new report two years later, Proba (2013) applied the same method to conclude that for five other social security schemes the total magnitude of fraud might be 5 percent of the total payments from the government (parental 3.2 percent, unemployment 4.1 percent, disability 4.5 percent, work assessment allowance 6.6 percent, and transitional to single parents 12.8 percent). Proba then multiplied the yearly expenses with the assumed fraud percentage for each social security scheme. Its approach resulted in an estimated 6 billion NOK ($0.75 billion) for the five schemes and 2 billion NOK ($0.25 billion) for sick pay, totaling 8 billion NOK ($1 billion).

Based on the total amounts that were paid under these benefits (194 billion NOK) Proba's (2013) estimate of the total social security fraud in 2015 amounted to as much as 9.8 billion NOK, or 5.1 percent of the total payments under the six schemes. This is a very high figure and Proba emphasizes that there are large uncertainties in its estimate. The introduction to their 2013 report states that:

> ...if we add up the estimated amounts that are the result of fraudulent behavior, we find that 5 percent of the total expenses for the five schemes are probably subject to fraud. We should note that these estimates are higher than what the experts think is most likely. The reason is that they see a clear risk that the correct figure is higher than the number they think is most likely.

As a measure of this uncertainty, Proba (2013) indicates where expert limits are found in terms of 10 percent likelihood that the fraud fraction is

Table 8.1 Comparison of estimates for white-collar crime and social security fraud

	Variation in estimates	
	White-collar crime (billion NOK)	Social security fraud (billion NOK)
Detected crime	1.1	0.3
Low estimate	4.4	2.6
Main estimate	11.9	9.8
High estimate	56.8	21.9

lower or higher. The overall estimate of 5.1 percent is thus what the experts as a panel believe is most likely, with a minimum border of 1.4 percent and a maximum border of 11.3 percent, for fraud. Translated into monetary terms, these percentages suggest that the scope of social security fraud can be anywhere between 2.6 billion NOK and 21.9 billion NOK, see Table 8.1.

Another significant element of uncertainty in Proba's estimate is that there is a distinct gap between the perceptions of the various experts. For example, one expert said that the proportion of fraud in disability benefits is as high as 15 percent, while consensus among the other eight experts ranged from 2.5 percent to 5 percent. The Proba (2013) report points out that his one estimate is so extreme that it increases the average estimated fraud amount in this area from 3.2 percent to 4.5 percent, or by 1.1 billion NOK.

In 2015, NAV reported to the police 1472 people in 1559 cases who committed fraud totaling 303 million NOK. Almost all cases were in the six different support schemes mentioned above. NAV reported cases of 200,000 NOK on average to the police. This is in contrast to white-collar crime cases, each of several million NOK. Most social security fraud was related to unemployment benefits (121 million NOK in total) and work assessment allowance (98 million NOK in total).

Unemployment benefits and transitional benefits were the two schemes with the largest fraction of total police reports that year (0.9 percent of all recipients). Overall, the reported cases constituted as little as 0.15 percent of total disbursements in 2015. So this is the tip of the iceberg, or the known size, when it comes to social security fraud of 0.3 billion NOK.

Meanwhile, we recall that the experts Proba polled were of the opinion that the fraud proportion is 5.1 percent, or more than 30 times higher.

For disability benefit and parental benefit schemes, the experts estimated that the fraud is over 200 times greater than the amount actually reported by NAV to the police. In other words, Proba's (2013) expert panel suggest that the magnitude of the invisible part of the iceberg is enormous, and that NAV only manages to capture a very small proportion of the fraud that it believes is actually occurring.

In addition to the expert panel, Proba (2013) also carried out survey research among employees at NAV. The purpose was to compare and support expert estimates. When asked what percentage of swindlers they think is discovered, they responded on average with 11 percent for the six schemes. This results in fraud of only 2.7 billion NOK ($0.3 \times 100 / 11$). The sum of 2.7 billion NOK from survey research can be compared to 9.8 billion NOK from expert elicitation. An iceberg tip of 11 percent for social security fraud can also be compared to an iceberg tip of 9.4 percent for white-collar crime.

If 11 percent is indeed a relevant estimate (and the reported amount is equal to only 0.15 percent of total security payments under the six schemes), then this result indicates that the real fraud is in the order of 1.4 percent, or just over one-quarter of the expert panel's estimate in the same report by Proba (2013). Conversely, if the experts estimate that the scam is over 30 times greater than what is reported to the police, this implicitly means that NAV in its detection does not reach 11 percent, but achieves only 3 percent. The implication is either that the NAV detection fraction is extremely low or that the expert panel provided unrealistically high estimates.

The survey research also revealed that some NAV employees see a bandit in nearly every beneficiary. When asked what percentage of those receiving disability benefits and work assessment allowance "do not meet the requirements or knowingly violate the rules", several respondents indicated that as many as 30, 40, or 50 percent of recipients might fit this description.

Admittedly, NAV demanded an additional 1.2 billion NOK in 2015 to be paid back by beneficiaries, in addition to the 300 million NOK reported to the police. The 1.2 billion NOK is made up of numerous, smaller, fraud cases that are not reported to the police. The incorrect payments are caused by the user, but not necessarily because of gross negligence or intention to commit social security fraud.

Some may argue that the visible part of the iceberg is not just 300 million NOK, but 1.2 billion NOK, and then the expert estimate from Proba (2013) emerges as more realistic. However, there is no exact method to indicate what part of the claimed amount of 1.2 billion NOK should be taken into account as part of the iceberg tip in this case.

A different estimate in 2013 was calculated by consultants from SAS Institute who ended up with a total of 2 billion NOK of social security fraud in Norway. In addition, they found 8 billion NOK that was caused by system and procedural errors at NAV. The total of 10 billion NOK is very similar to Proba's 9.8 billion NOK, but with the major difference being that incorrect payments were caused by NAV rather than by fraud committed by social security recipients.

"Ten billion is an unimaginably large amount", the secretary for employment in Norway is reported to have said, "It goes without saying that we have much to gain by strengthening efforts to combat social security fraud."

However, as it turned out, according to SAS Institute, 8 out of the 10 billion NOK was caused by social security service error and not by the recipients. In essence, there were system and procedural errors at NAV accounting for the majority of misconduct. Rather than pursue even relatively small amounts all the way through the court system, NAV should instead strengthen efforts to combat fraud by improving its internal practices.

Internal malpractice at NAV was highlighted in the fall of 2016. Media reports stated that "the public prosecutor is investigating the NAV scandal", "notifications and whistleblowers were ignored", and social security recipients "could have avoided jail". This is indeed worrying, especially given that the fraction of reports from NAV that were dismissed by the police had been reduced from 24 percent in 2011 to 15 percent in 2015. Out of all fraud cases brought in front of a judge, almost all (97.3 percent) led to convictions in 2015. Many convicts might have been innocent.

Since 2002, NAV has accused about 1,300 individuals of unemployment benefit fraud involving falsely high amounts. Police investigators and state prosecutors have relied blindly on figures from NAV and prosecuted individuals for social security fraud based on these amounts. An inquiry conducted in 2017 by the Norwegian attorney general concluded that more than 600 individuals had been sentenced severely. Many had been sentenced too severely, and many were unlawfully sentenced to community service rather than just paying a fine.

White-collar criminals and their attorneys would never accept such accusations from authorities without even being able to control and challenge claims.

The review above shows that there is a legitimate question to ask: Is the estimate for annual social security fraud of about 10 billion NOK too high? But this number is the only one that NAV has in terms of metrics in this area, and therefore the figure lives on in the public's mind.

Although the 9.8 billion NOK ($1.2 billion) is enormous in a small nation like Norway, we suggest that the value for white-collar crime is even larger. So the magnitude itself should not be the issue. When the police prioritize hundreds and thousands of small-scale economic crime cases like social security fraud, then there tends to be few police resources left to investigate large-scale economic crime cases. While social security fraud cases are concerned with the equivalent of less than $50,000 each, large-scale white-collar crime cases are valued at several million dollars each.

The victim of social security fraud is always the community ultimately. Victims of white-collar crime are a mixed group, such as employers, banks, customers, and the community. In criminal law, all victims are equally important.

Social Conflict Theory

Social conflict theory suggests that the powerful and wealthy in the upper class of society define what is right and what is wrong. The rich and mighty can behave like "robber barons" because they make the laws. Therefore, the ruling class does not consider a white-collar offense as a regular crime, and certainly not one similar to street crime. Why would the powerful punish their own?

Social conflict theory views financial crime as a function of the conflict that exists in society (Siegel 2011). The theory suggests that class conflict causes crime in any society, and that those in power create laws to protect their rights and interests. For example, embezzlement by employees is a violation of law to protect the interests of the employer. However, it might be argued that an employer must and should protect its own assets. Bank fraud is a crime to protect the powerful banking sector. However, from the perspective of conflict theory one might argue that a bank should have systems in place making bank fraud impossible and suffers if it does not. If an employee has no opportunity to commit embezzlement, and if a fraudster has no opportunity to commit bank fraud, then these kinds of financial crime would never occur, and there would be no need to have laws against such offenses. Law enforcement protects powerful companies against counterfeit products, although they should be able to protect themselves by reducing opportunities for the production of such products.

Social conflict theory holds that laws and law enforcement are used by dominant groups in society to minimize threats to their interests posed by those whom they perceive as dangerous and greedy (Petrocelli et al. 2003). Crime is defined by legal codes and sanctioned by institutions of criminal justice to secure order in society. The ruling class secures order in the ruled class by means of laws and law enforcement. Conflicts and clashes between interest groups are restrained and stabilized by law enforcement (Schwendinger and Schwendinger 2014).

According to social conflict theory, the justice system is biased and designed to protect the wealthy and powerful. The wealthy and powerful can take substantial assets out of their own companies at their own discretion whenever they like, although employed workers in the companies are the ones who create the value. The super-rich can exploit the wealth that they have created as owners of corporations as long as they do not hurt other shareholders and employees have no right to object. It is no crime to take out value from one's own enterprise and build private mansions with the money. Even when owners have simply inherited wealth created by earlier generations, they can use it freely for private consumption. Similarly, top executives who are on each other's corporate boards grant each other salaries that are 10–20 times higher than regular employee salaries. As Haines (2014: 21) puts it, "financial practices that threaten corporate interests, such as embezzlement, are clearly identified as criminal even as obscenely high salaries remain relatively untouched by regulatory controls". Furthermore, sharp practices such as insider trading that threaten confidence in equities markets have enjoyed vigorous prosecution, since the powerful see them as opaque transactions that give an unfair advantage to those who are not members of the market institutions.

Karl Marx who analyzed capitalism and suggested the transition to socialism and ultimately to communism, created the basis for social conflict theory. Capitalism is an economic system in which persons privately own trade, industries, firms, shops, and means of production and operate these enterprises for profit. Socialism is an economic system characterized by cooperative enterprises, common ownership, and state ownership. Communism is a socio-economic system structured upon the common ownership of the means of production and characterized by the absence of social class.

Marxist criminology views the competitive nature of the capitalist system as a major cause of financial crime (Siegel 2011). It focuses on what creates stability and continuity in society, and it adopts a pre-defined political philosophy. Marxist criminology focuses on why things change by identifying the disruptive forces in capitalist societies, and describing how power, wealth, prestige, and perceptions of the world divide every society. The economic struggle is the central venue for the Marxists. Marx divided society into two unequal classes and demonstrated the inequality in the historical transition from patrician and slave to capitalist and wage worker: this is the rulers versus the ruled. Marx also underlined that all societies have a certain hierarchy wherein a higher class has more privileges than a lower one. In a capitalist society where economic resources equate to power, it is in the interest of the ascendant class to maintain economic stratification in order to dictate the legal order (Petrocelli et al. 2003).

McKeever (2012) suggests that those who are socially, economically, and politically vulnerable are those who typically benefit from the social security system. Social security fraud can vary from sophisticated, organized, and large-scale offenses to minor, low level frauds committed by individual claimants. While the money gained through a minor fraud is relatively small, the cumulative amount lost to low level fraud constitutes a significant sum (Ceccato and Benson 2016).

When studying relatively minor social security fraud committed by individual claimants, McKeever (2012) found that the legal response to these frauds in both the UK and Australia is quite harsh. She suggests that a new policy framework is required, within which low level fraud is decriminalized. She argues that at present, minor fraud is so broadly defined that it encompasses as a norm behavior that does not uniformly meet proper standards of criminal culpability, pulling into its path claimants who have not intentionally and dishonestly committed fraud.

In contrast to this view, social conflict theory explains why the ruling class will never allow the decriminalization of social security fraud. It will never accept the view that minor fraud prosecution represents a form of overcriminalization targeted at the losers in society.

An illustration of the class perspective is the extent to which the police start investigating reported cases of social security fraud compared to white-collar crime such as bankruptcy cases. The police in Oslo start investigations into 85 percent of all cases reported by NAV, but only 10 percent of all cases reported by bankruptcy attorneys (Solem 2016).

Evasion of social security contributions can set disincentives for people to return to the official labor markets. Instead, benefit abusers become engaged in the shadow economy (Petersen et al. 2010).

Social conflict theory suggests that laws and regulations are implemented by the elite to control others in society. However, to stay in charge, the elite does have to punish their own sometimes. An example of a convicted white-collar criminal in Norway was presented in this book. When compared to another example in this book—a convicted social security fraudster—it seems that the sentencing varies depending on class. The social security fraudster was sentenced to a slightly longer prison term although the white-collar criminal had committed a more serious crime in terms of the amount of money involved in his offense.

References

Agder. (2015, September 30). Case LA-2015-195071, *Agder lagmannsrett* [Agder Court of Appeals].

Brooks, G., & Button, M. (2011). The Police and Fraud Investigation and the Case for a Nationalized Solution in the United Kingdom. *The Police Journal, 84*, 305–319.

Ceccato, V., & Benson, M. L. (2016). Tax Evasion in Sweden 2002–2013: Interpreting Changes in the Rot/Rut Deduction System and Predicting Future Trends. *Crime, Law and Social Change, 66*, 217–232.

Haines, F. (2014). Corporate Fraud as Misplaced Confidence? Exploring Ambiguity in the Accuracy of Accounts and the Materiality of Money. *Theoretical Criminology, 18*(1), 20–37.

Kynn, M. (2008). The 'Heuristics and Biases' Bias in Expert Elicitation. *Journal of the Royal Statistical Society, 171*, 239–264.

Lensvelt-Mulders, G. J. L. M., Heijden, P. G. M., & Laudy, O. (2006). A Validation of a Computer-Assisted Randomized Response Survey to Estimate the Prevalence of Fraud in Social Security. *Journal of the Royal Statistical Society, 169*, 305–318.

McKeever, G. (2012). Social Citizenship and Social Security Fraud in the UK and Australia. *Social Policy & Administration, 46*(4), 465–482.

Petersen, H. G., Thiessen, U., & Wohlleben, P. (2010). Shadow Economy, Tax Evasion, and Transfer Fraud – Definition, Measurement, and Data Problems. *International Economic Journal, 24*(4), 421–441.

Petrocelli, M., Piquero, A. R., & Smith, M. R. (2003). Conflict Theory and Racial Profiling: An Empirical Analysis of Police Traffic Stop Data. *Journal of Criminal Justice, 31*, 1–11.

Proba. (2011). *Misbruk av sykepengeordningen i folketrygden* [Abuse of Sick Pay Scheme in National Insurance]. Oslo: Proba samfunnsanalyse.

Proba. (2013). *Trygdesvindel i Norge: En kartlegging av fem stønadsordninger* [Social Security Fraud in Norway: A Survey of Five Support Areas]. Oslo: Proba samfunnsanalyse.

Schwendinger, H., & Schwendinger, J. (2014). Defenders of Order or Guardians of Human Rights? *Social Justice, 40*(1/2), 87–117.
Siegel, L. J. (2011). *Criminology* (11th ed.). Belmont: Wadsworth Publishing.
Solem, L. K. (2016, September 25 Friday). *Kan slippe med 10 måneder i fengsel* [Can Get Away with 10 Months in Prison]. Daily Norwegian Business Newspaper *Dagens Næringsliv*, pp. 12–13.
Sutherland, E. H. (1939). White-Collar Criminality. *American Sociological Review, 5*, 1–12.

Open Access This chapter is licensed under the terms of the Creative Commons Attribution 4.0 International License (http://creativecommons.org/licenses/by/4.0/), which permits use, sharing, adaptation, distribution and reproduction in any medium or format, as long as you give appropriate credit to the original author(s) and the source, provide a link to the Creative Commons license and indicate if changes were made.

The images or other third party material in this chapter are included in the chapter's Creative Commons license, unless indicated otherwise in a credit line to the material. If material is not included in the chapter's Creative Commons license and your intended use is not permitted by statutory regulation or exceeds the permitted use, you will need to obtain permission directly from the copyright holder.

CHAPTER 9

Other Macroeconomic Estimations

Abstract White-collar crime is part of the shadow economy. The shadow economy may be any kind of illegal activity that causes damage to the financial interests of the country, performed by legal and illegal businesses. Just like the magnitude of white-collar crime cannot be specifically observed, the shadow economy is generally not observable, so its magnitude must be estimated. This can be done either by direct procedures at a microlevel, by indirect procedures that make use of macroeconomic indicators, or with statistical models to estimate the shadow economy. Given the uncertainty in all macroeconomic estimates of crime—be it white-collar crime, tax evasion, or social security fraud—it is extremely important to be cautious in the application of such numbers in political and management arguments.

Keywords Gabriel Zucman • Hidden wealth • Labor market crime • MIMIC approach • Money laundering • Offshore accounts • Panama Papers • Shadow economy • Tax evasion • Tax haven

White-collar crime is part of the shadow economy. The shadow economy is defined as the market-based production of goods and services, whether legal or illegal, that escapes detection in the official estimates of gross domestic product (GDP). The shadow economy comprises those economic activities and the income derived from them that circumvent or otherwise avoid government regulation, taxation, or observation (Schneider and Williams 2013).

The shadow economy is sometimes labeled the informal economy (Edelbacher et al. 2016: 1):

> The informal economy is emerging worldwide as an antipode to the formal economy. Although only partially visible and parallel to the formal economic system, it is manifested in social and cultural activities in European cities in the tourist trade, in the form of vendors in the streets and squares or those selling flowers in restaurants. It has links to drug trafficking and prostitution, but also provides economic opportunities for immigrants, young people, and students. It has links with the formal economy, contributes to the forces of formal and informal social control, and is an important factor in the economies of European countries.

The shadow economy is illegal economic or non-complying economic activity within legal businesses existing alongside a country's official and legitimate economy, for example, transactions such as underdeclared income, undeclared work and overdeclared costs. The shadow economy is sometimes labeled the underground economy. It may be any kind of illegal activity that causes damage to the financial interests of the country, performed by legal and illegal businesses.

Here are some elements of the shadow economy:

- Organized use of fictitious invoices: Issuance and filing of invoices where the actual delivery of goods or services is not according to the statement. In the organized use of fictitious invoices, several people and companies are cooperating in a network in order to appear legitimate.
- Undeclared income: Keeping revenue, or parts of revenue, away from the official financial statements, and thus knowingly avoiding reporting. Operators keep the value added tax (VAT) paid by customers by not passing it on to the government, and in addition, they are saving income tax on the generated profits.
- Cross-border money transfers: Transferring, hiding, and illegally securing acquired proceeds. This is related to the second stage of the money laundering process, in which proceeds are converted or moved to create a distance from the crime source and crime scene.

- Missing traders: Charging VAT when importing and selling goods, and subsequently disappearing without paying the tax to the government's collection authority. So-called "carousel fraud" is a method whereby goods are imported VAT free, but not sold for consumption in the relevant markets. Instead, the goods pass between several businesses, each of them liable to VAT, before being exported. The first link will often disappear without paying VAT, while the final link will reclaim VAT from the government.
- Misuse of companies: Establishing or changing the company as a concealment framework for illegal activities.
- Illegal workers: Using illegal workers often includes both illegal residence and illegal work, and can imply penalties for both the employer and the employee, if detected. A large demand for unreported employment and cheap labor seems to be an important driver.
- Use of legal business as shield: Hiding and laundering proceeds from the illegal economy.
- False identity for immigrants/refugees: Abusing identities includes false, stolen, or sold identity documents. Based on the application of incorrect information, false documents or documents belonging to another individual or a fake person, it may be possible to acquire a residence permit under false pretenses. False residence and work permits enable criminals to obtain employment, thereby causing the workplace to use illegal workers and pay wages under fraudulent social security numbers.

The main categories of white-collar crime include fraud, theft, manipulation, and corruption. When bank fraud is committed, bank costs increase, thereby reducing value creation in the bank. At the same time, the fraudster spends the illegal money. When theft is committed, organizational income decreases, thereby reducing value creation in the organization. At the same time, the thief consumes or uses the stolen goods and services. With manipulation, such as accounting manipulation, tax evasion may occur, which reduces government income. At the same time, the manipulator consumes or uses the withdrawn funds. With corruption, the values on the bribing side are reduced, while values on the bribed side are consumed or used.

The magnitude of white-collar crime cannot specifically be observed, and likewise the shadow economy is generally not observable, so its magnitude must be estimated (Breusch 2005). Schneider and Williams (2013) argue that there is no appropriate methodology to assess the scope of the shadow economy. Rather, there are three competing methods of assessment for the size of the shadow economy that are used:

1. Direct procedures at a micro level that aim to determine the size of the shadow economy at one particular point in time. An example is survey method.
2. Indirect procedures that make use of macroeconomic indicators in order to proxy the development of the shadow economy over time.
3. Statistical models that use statistical tools to estimate the shadow economy as an unobserved variable.

The most commonly used method of measurement is based on a combination of the multiple indicator multiple cause model (known as MIMIC) and the currency demand method. The MIMIC model assumes that the shadow economy remains an unobserved phenomenon which can be estimated using quantitatively measurable causes of shadow economic activity as well as indicators of illicit activity (Schneider and Williams 2013: 28):

> The causes will include variables such as the tax burden and the intensity of regulation, and the indicators will include variables such as the demand for currency, official national income figure and official working hours data. The econometric models are complex and have to deal with a range of well-known challenges such as endogeneity problems. For example, the size of the tax burden might make it more difficult for the government to raise taxes so it responds by raising tax rates and therefore the tax burden on the level of official national income.

The MIMIC model produces relative estimates of the size and development of the shadow economy. Typically, the shadow economy is estimated at around 14 percent in countries such as Norway. And 14 percent of GDP in Norway represents 420 billion NOK ($53 billion). In comparison, the shadow economy is estimated at 16 percent in Belgium, 14 percent in Sweden, 13 percent in Denmark and Germany, and 8 percent in Austria.

Petersen et al. (2010) suggest that the shadow economy can be identified as a single sector if a precise theoretical separation between sectors is made. If a clear concept of shadow activities is applied, the problem of tax evasion can also be identified in an appropriate way: tax evasion can take place in the market economy as well as in the shadow economy. The demarcation between criminal activities and shadow activities is of high relevance because the former does not positively contribute to total income or wealth while the latter can.

Evans (2016) suggests that viewed in a wider context of paid and unpaid informal economic activities, the shadow economy highlights four categories of economic activity:

1. Illegal economic activity: Generating goods and services that are forbidden by law and/or are unlawful when provided by unauthorized producers.
2. Paid informal economic activity: An activity that is hidden and thus not registered with or by the state, but the goods and services provided through it are otherwise deemed legal.
3. Self-provisioning: An activity that is undertaken by household members for themselves and/or for other household members.
4. Mutual aid: An activity carried out by household members for members of other households in the wider community.

Schneider et al. (2010) estimated the magnitude and development of the shadow economy all over the world, and the results for a few nations are listed in Table 9.1. The shadow economy in Norway exhibits a declining fraction of GDP from 19.2 percent in 1999 to 18.0 percent in 2007. Two comparable nations have similar results.

Schneider et al. (2010) suggest that the weighted average size of the shadow economy as a percentage of official GDP in Sub-Saharan Africa is 38.4 percent, in Europe and Central Asia it is 36.5 percent, and in high-income OECD countries (such as Norway) 13.5 percent.

The GDP in Norway is above 3 trillion NOK. In another application of MIMIC in 2017, the total magnitude of labor market crime was estimated.

Table 9.1 Shadow economy as a fraction (%) of GDP (Schneider et al. 2010)

Country	1999	2000	2001	2002	2003	2004	2005	2006	2007
Norway	19.2	19.1	19.0	19.0	19.0	18.5	18.5	18.2	18.0
Switzerland	8.8	8.6	8.6	8.6	8.8	8.6	8.5	8.3	8.1
Sweden	19.6	19.2	19.1	19.0	18.7	18.5	18.6	18.2	17.9

Labor market crime means all kinds of financial crime related to the supply of and demand for labor, such as social security fraud and tax evasion. Labor market crime is a violation of the law concerning wages and working conditions, social security, VAT, and tax evasion; organized crime contributes to the minimization of the production costs of goods and services and thus undermines social structures and distorts competition.

It was estimated in Norway by Samfunnsøkonomisk analyse (2017) that labor market crime represents more than 4 percent of GDP, thereby resulting in a total fraud of 95 billion NOK ($12 billion). We return to this study below.

The Washington-based organization Global Financial Integrity (GFI) estimates that transnational crime is a $1.6 trillion to $2.2 trillion annual illegal business. However, there is no explicit methodology used to arrive at this enormous figure. Rather, it is the sum of many figures that are updated without any methodological explanations. In part, there are some observations that are multiplied by the likelihood of detection, such as the illegal arms trade.

The MIMIC Model

We have applied a bottom-up approach by expert elicitation for estimating the magnitude of white-collar crime. An alternative approach might be a top-down approach using econometric modeling where it is assumed that traces and evidence of white-collar crime can be found in the macroeconomy. One econometric modeling approach uses the MIMIC model, which is frequently applied to estimate the magnitude of the underground economy in society. It is an indirect approach using macroeconomic indicators as a proxy for the size of the underground economy (Imamoglu 2016). MIMIC has been exposed to serious criticism. For example, Breusch (2005) argues that the method is subjective and pliable in practice and thus unfit for the purpose of estimating unknown sizes such as the magnitude of the underground economy.

The MIMIC model might have been applied to our estimation of white-collar crime. One way would be to study the effect of additional control activities and see how much more crime was detected. This is an approach that has been applied in Norway not to estimate the magnitude of white-collar crime, but to estimate the magnitude of financial crime related to the labor market. We present the labor market study as follows.

In step 1, a selection model is estimated that indicates the probability that an actor is selected for control related to labor market crime. In step 2, a model is estimated that indicates the likelihood that the actor commits labor market crime, while at the same time correction for selection bias is introduced. In 2014, there were 976,372 business organizations in Norway that might be controlled; 3,025 business were selected for control and controlled. Among these businesses, 4.63 percent were caught committing labor marked crime.

Based on this fraction, Samfunnsøkonomisk analyse (2017) estimated that the total magnitude of labor market crime in Norway is 95 billion NOK ($12 billion).

MIMIC models are being used to estimate the size of the underground economy or the tax gap in various countries by applying structural equations. There are two kinds of observed variables in the model—causal variables and indicator variables—which are connected by a black box of unobservable factors. The challenge is first to estimate the contents of the black box.

The black box is typically estimated by a microanalysis. For example, microdata at the business level from the tax administration agency can be used to estimate the likelihood that an enterprise is conducting criminal offenses related to taxes and fees. The idea is that certain combinations of characteristics of businesses coincide with a higher probability of occupational crime than other characteristics.

An obvious weakness of these data is that they are not representative of populations, as controls are not conducted in a random selection. However, it is possible to use an estimation method developed to control the selectivity of the sample and thus find a likelihood of crime for all businesses.

The probability that an actor will get caught for tax evasion can be used to predict the extent of work-life crime, given different characteristics, such as industry or geographical area. Information from the internal revenue service as the tax authority (e.g., the Norwegian Tax Administration) can provide insights into characteristics of businesses that commit tax fraud and be used to estimate the extent of this kind of crime.

The process can be that the tax administration's overview of controlled businesses allows a mapping of the characteristics of the businesses that were taken for labor-related transactions in tax evasion. This information is then used to estimate the true visibility of a given activity in the population of all Norwegian companies involved in tax and tax crime. Furthermore, based on observed crime rates for those actually checked and on predicted crime rates for those not checked, it is possible to calculate average rates for the entire population.

A main problem with such a data set is that controls that are carried out are not random. The selection of control objects is risk-based, and controlled businesses are therefore not a representative sample of the population. To say something about the likelihood that those undetected by control actually perform illegal activities similar to those detected by control weakens the quality of the basis. Thus, a relevant variable is the non-detected businesses after control.

Factors that may affect the likelihood of labor-related deviant actions largely coincide with factors that influence control selection, as one wishes to control non-compliant actors. This contributes to skewness in the results. Such a skewed selection may provide incorrect an estimation and conclusion as to what may be relevant areas of action. This also allows for adjustments by business actors, because it can give an impression of what characteristics typically lead to control, thus allowing deviant actors to avoid standing out just on these criteria.

When the likelihood of control depends on factors that the offender may influence, such as recorded income, then the offender can influence the likelihood of detection. By providing a reported income that does not deviate too much from others in its industry, a business may have a low probability of being caught for tax evasion.

Randomized controls provide more valid results. A randomized control was conducted in Denmark, where the study concludes that the rate of tax avoidance is low. A key question in the study is: Are rules being followed because there is no possibility of evasion or whether there is a desire to act lawfully? The study found that a very small proportion (0.3 percent) of those who were not responsible for reporting their own income to the authorities were cheating, while a large proportion (37 percent) of those who had their own responsibility to report income were cheating. Overall, the study concludes that the monetary amount lost to tax cheating is small.

Breusch (2005: 22) studied three applications of MIMIC and asked whether MIMC models are appropriate:

> The MIMIC model has its origins in the factor analysis of psychometrics, where the correlations of observable variables are explained by common factors or unobservable latent variables. Whether or not a statistical model is suited to a particular application is to some extent a question of judgment, but there are extensions of the original psychometric factor model where the MIMIC structure seems natural.

Breusch (2005: 23) argues that two MIMIC implications—alternative measurements of the same thing and lack of correlation between causes and latent variable—are problematic:

> Both of these implications are unacceptable in the applications being considered here (the shadow economy). The first suggests that observed GDP and currency holdings are related to the various causal factors in the model – tax rates, unemployment rates, government expenditures, etc. – only through the size of the underground economy. Such a proposition is inconsistent with every known macroeconomic theory of income determination. The second proposition is equally implausible because it says that currency holdings are unrelated to observed income, once account is taken of the underground economy. If nothing else, that arrangement contradicts the currency demand model used in each of these studies to derive a benchmark value for calibrating the index from the MIMIC model.

Macroeconomic estimations are based on causality among variables. For example, many researchers assume that there is a causal relationship between unemployment rates and economic crime rates (e.g., Altindag 2012). They assume that higher unemployment rates cause higher economic crime rates. But it is not at all certain that this causality exists. Several researchers have questioned the use of unemployment rates as explanatory factors in econometric studies which address the relationship between the economy and crime (Yearwood and Koinis 2011).

For example, Yearwood and Koinis (2011) studied and tested the efficacy of the unemployment rate for predicting the reported property crime rate and to identify other economic indicators which may also prove to be useful for predicting crime rates with financial motives. Specifically, they looked at theft, burglary, robbery, fraud, and embezzlement. Given the exploratory nature of their research, seven stepwise regressions were computed with unemployment emerging as a significant predictor for only one of the criminal offenses. Research findings from their study identified alternative causal variables, such as average wage and salary disbursements, supplemental security income receipts, the consumer price index, and per capita personal income.

Yearwood and Koinis (2011) illustrate with their research how important it is to critically examine the use of unemployment rates and other variables in macroeconomic estimations of financial crime. While it certainly seems intuitively and theoretically plausible to assume that more unemployment causes more economic crime—simply because unemployed people must find economic means to serve their material needs—it is important to have a sound empirical as well as theoretical basis before causality is introduced in macroeconomic estimations.

In empirical terms, the unemployment rate proved to be neither a sufficient nor a statistically significant measure in six of Yearwood and Koinis' (2011) seven regression models. While Cebula (2012) argues that Yearwood and Koinis' (2011) models suffer from misspecification problems, it is nevertheless worth emphasizing that jumping on intuitively attractive causal relationships for variables that are easily available in public national statistics is simply not very smart in econometrics.

MAGNITUDE OF MONEY LAUNDERING

Hendriyetty and Grewal (2017) studied the magnitude of money laundering in the world. Money laundering occurs when criminals try to conceal their proceeds of crime by deleting their tracks in financial systems, international trade, or through other efforts. Actions to conceal these proceeds, or funds derived from criminal acts, are intended to conceal the origin of the property so that it can appear legitimate. Money laundering is a global concern as it has significantly negative effects on the economies of both developed and developing countries.

The most widely quoted figure for the extent of money laundering is the International Monetary Fund's (IMF's) estimate of 2–5 percent of world GDP. An estimate for Austria is 1.2–1.8 percent, while another estimate is 6.5 percent in Europe. Hendriyetty and Grewal (2017) argue that measuring the extent of money laundering is extremely complex, and it is therefore necessary to calculate from a range of viewpoints according to the approaches used by criminals. They argue that the safest way for money launderers to conceal their proceeds of crime is to send the money out of the jurisdiction, so capital flows between countries associated with money laundering can be mistakenly defined as capital flight.

Therefore, Hendriyetty and Grewal (2017) suggest estimating the magnitude of money laundering based on capital flight. They list five approaches: the hot money method, the residual approach, the Dooley method, trade misinvoicing and illicit financial flows. The first approach—the hot money method—measures capital flight used as a short-term capital export by financial institutions. Capital flight is calculated by measuring private capital flows, taking the errors and omissions and private short-term capital accounts from the balance of payments. This type of capital flight is defined as "hot money" because it arises as a quick response to economic conditions.

As pointed out by Hendriyetty and Grewal (2017), there are major differences between money laundering and capital flight, especially in policy and monitoring processes. Money laundering occurs because criminals send their money abroad to avoid detection by law enforcement agencies. Capital flight occurs to avoid the jurisdiction applied to capital or foreign exchange control.

The second approach is the residual approach, where capital flight is measured as the sum of gross capital inflows and the current account deficit, less increases in official foreign reserves. Capital flight is estimated by measuring the difference between inflows and outflows. The third approach is the Dooley method which proposes capital flight as an offset of the stock claims held by non-residents that do not generate investment income. The fourth approach is trade misinvoicing involving the measurement of deviance in export and import invoicing. The fifth approach looks at illicit money flows from developing countries.

Hendriyetty and Grewal (2017) suggest economic approaches as an alternative to capital flight to estimate the magnitude of money laundering. Micro- and macroeconomic approaches include tax evasion as a basis for estimating money laundering.

Magnitude of Tax Evasion

Ceccato and Benson (2016) studied the effects of changes in tax policy in Sweden as a case study of tax evasion. They use the term "tax gap", which refers to the difference between the taxes that were actually paid to the government in a particular reporting period and what should have been paid according to the rules determined by tax agency controls. The tax gap in Sweden is assumed to be 9 percent.

Ceccato and Benson (2016: 218) apply situational crime prevention theory to study tax evasion:

> Like rational choice theory and routine activity theory, situational crime prevention theory is part of what has been called the "opportunity" perspective on crime. The opportunity perspective first appeared on the criminological landscape four decades ago. In a nutshell, the opportunity perspective holds that opportunity is a fundamental cause of crime. The perspective assumes that individuals make choices to engage or not engage in crime

based on the availability and attractiveness of criminal opportunities. Situational crime prevention theory seeks to identify the factors that influence the distribution and attractiveness of criminal opportunities and then to suggest ways in which attractiveness might be reduced. The theory predicts that reducing the attractiveness of criminal opportunities will lead to reductions in crime.

Based on situational crime prevention theory, Ceccato and Benson (2016) study how changes in tax policy in Sweden affect individuals' and companies' motivations for tax evasion. In 2015, changes in the Swedish tax policy effectively raised certain taxes and reduced tax discounts, and thereby made tax evasion more attractive to potential tax evaders. For example, one allowable deduction for so-called "rot services" (household/renovation services) was reduced from 50 percent to 30 percent of labor costs, with a maximum discount of 50,000 SEK per annum. A more generous tax deduction would mean that a series of situational conditions favorable to tax avoidance would diminish. When changes in tax policy reduce rewards associated with evasion, then the reward versus risk equation is altered for the potential tax evader.

Ceccato and Benson (2016: 229) make specific predictions regarding future trends in tax evasion.

> Specifically, we predict that (1) if the Swedish Tax Agency does nothing except enforce the Rut/Rot tax as it has in the past and (2) if it continues to conduct the same surveys that it did between 2002 and 2013, then (3) a decrease in the indicators of tax compliance will be observed. The decrease will be more pronounced in some industries than in others, in particular construction, transportation, and hotels/restaurants.

Ceccato and Benson (2016) confirm that it is difficult to say how quickly tax compliance will fall and how great the decrease will be.

Shadow Economy and Market Activities

Petersen et al. (2010) present no estimate of the shadow economy. Rather, they try to shed some light on the definition of the shadow economy, in order to separate shadow activities from market activities and household production. They argue that the currency approach is not a promising concept for the estimation of the size of the shadow economy, since the factual influence of criminal activities on the money demand is unknown.

Petersen et al. (2010: 429) suggest that tax evasion and transfer fraud go hand-in-hand:

Shadow income and transfers then often constitute a net real income (from transfers, shadow activities and household production) that is considerably higher than the respective person would be able to earn in the official labor markets: the reservation wage mentioned in the introduction then functions as a poverty trap, detaining people from a return into the market economy. Tax evasion and transfer fraud go hand-in-hand, making poverty an ever-persisting phenomenon, which also creates some jobs in the 'welfare industries', where the engaged people are always complaining about a permanently rising gap in between 'the poor' and 'the rich' and increasing poverty – thus, guaranteeing them even more work for the coming generations.

Petersen et al. (2010) suggest that tax evasion can be defined and identified in the market sector, and it is usually taking place in the shadow economy, where it is often accompanied by evasion of social security contributions as well as transfer fraud.

Magnitude of Hidden Wealth

Andersen et al. (2017: 2) estimate that 15 percent of the windfall gains accruing to petroleum-producing countries with autocratic rulers are diverted to secret accounts:

> Political elites can abuse public office, or connections to those in the office, for private gain, and the struggle for state resources can have severe consequences in terms of political and economic instability.

Their dataset included country-level information about foreign-owned deposits in all significant financial centers including a number of important havens: jurisdictions that specialize in secrecy and asset protection such as Switzerland, Luxembourg, Cayman Islands, and Singapore. Their dataset constitutes a source of information on hidden wealth.

Andersen et al.'s (2017: 3) finding is that petroleum windfalls translate into significant increases in hidden wealth, but only when institutional checks and balances are weak:

> Specifically, we estimate that a doubling of the oil price causes a 22 percent increase in haven deposits owned by petroleum-rich autocracies, corresponding to almost 1.5 percent of GDP at the sample mean, whereas there is no such effect on haven deposits owned by petroleum-rich non-autocracies.

Since a doubling of the oil price is associated with an estimated 10 percent increase in the GDP of petroleum-rich countries, the result suggests that around 15 percent of the windfall gains accruing to countries with autocratic rulers is diverted to offshore accounts.

To establish the link between hidden wealth and political elites more firmly, Andersen et al. (2017) studied how tax haven deposits evolve in periods of increased political uncertainty. They found that haven deposits owned by autocracies start increasing significantly a few quarters before elections, suggesting that political elites anticipate the political risk inherent in elections and respond by hiding wealth in havens.

The methodological challenge facing this research was theoretical explanations for correlation and regression analysis. For example, income was correlated with hidden savings, while the regression was concerned with sham structures. As Andersen et al. (2017) point out themselves, it may be suspected that the correlation between petroleum rents and haven deposits is related to the presence of multinational firms in the petroleum industry. Through transfer pricing and thin capitalization, multinational firms shift taxable profits to havens, making developing countries vulnerable to tax avoidance. This may suggest an alternative explanation for the suggestion that oil and gas rents transferred to havens belong to multinational firms rather than domestic elites.

An editor in a Norwegian newspaper criticized estimates from Andersen et al. (2017) by refusing the claim that super-rich people pay little or no tax (Hegnar 2017: 2):

> It has been speculated and researched how much is being avoided in taxation. Good numbers have not been received. There are mostly rough estimates of how much of GDP is assumed to be avoided and how much of the tax revenue it constitutes. A popular exercise in Norway has been using numbers from other countries (for example 5 percent or 10 percent of GDP) and apply this on Norwegian GDP, and thus there have been bombastic claims about tax evasion for several hundred billion kroner.
>
> The hopelessness of these exercises is, for example, using numbers from a country like Italy, with a 25 percent unemployment rate, and comparing with Norway with an unemployment rate of 3–4 percent. It must be wrong. In a country where almost 70 percent are in work, and where the public sector is large and the benefits are high, it is less tax evasion than in Italy and similar countries.

While we will return to the issue of abuse of macroeconomic estimates, it is interesting to note that both *The Economist* and the *Guardian* quote the same numbers. *The Economist* had the following headlines: "The super-rich are different: they pay less tax" and "The Swiss leaks and Panama papers open a window on the tax dodger's world". The *Guardian* had the following headlines: "Super-rich evade on average nearly third of their due tax" and "Chance of assets being hidden rises very sharply with wealth, finds economists' study based on Panama Papers data".

Wealth Held in Offshore Accounts

Switzerland has, starting from the end of World War I, held a unique position amongst the world's centers of wealth management. Today, one-third of the world's offshore wealth is held there (Zucman 2015: 36). Other well-known tax havens such as the City of London, Hong Kong, Singapore, Jersey, Cayman Islands, Bahamas, and Luxembourg have emerged in the last couple of decades, following the same basic recipe as Switzerland (Zucman 2015: 23):

> In all these tax havens, private bankers do the same things as in Geneva: they hold stock and bond portfolios for their foreign customers, collect dividends and interest, provide investment advice as well as other services, such as the possibility of having a current account that earns little or nothing. And, thanks to the limited forms of cooperation with foreign tax authorities, they all offer the same service that is in high demand: the possibility of not paying any taxes on dividends, interest, capital gains, wealth, or inheritances.

Zucman (2015) estimates that on a global scale households owned 8 percent of their financial wealth through bank accounts in tax havens in 2014, amounting to $7.6 trillion. For Europe alone, the estimated share is 10 percent, or $2.6 trillion. This fraud translates into a conservative estimate for lost tax revenues for the world as a whole of $190 billion annually. Zucman's estimate is considerably lower than a previous estimate made by James Henry from the Tax Justice Network (Henry 2012), claiming that between $21 and $32 trillion was invested through the world's still expanding "black hole" of more than 80 tax havens. Both estimates look at financial wealth, in other words the sum of all the bank deposits, portfolios of stocks and bonds, shares in mutual funds, and insurance contracts held by individuals throughout the world, net of any debt.

They must be considered lower bounds for the actual wealth accumulated by the super-rich. Zucman (2015: 44–45) notes that his estimate does not include real estate in foreign countries, or non-financial wealth like works of art, jewelry and gold stashed anonymously in repositories in places like Geneva, Luxembourg and Singapore:

> High net-worth individuals also own real estate in foreign countries: islands in the Seychelles, chalets in Gstaad, and so on. Registry data show that a large chunk of London's luxury real estate is held through shell companies, largely domiciled in the British Virgin Islands, a scheme that enables owners to remain anonymous and to exploit tax loopholes. Unfortunately, there is no way yet to estimate the value of such real assets held abroad.

Zucman's estimate of hidden financial wealth is made by examining anomalies in the balance sheets that record the assets and liabilities between countries. Zucman (2015: 37) gives the following example:

> [L]et's imagine a British person who holds in her Swiss bank account a portfolio of American securities—for example, stock in Google. What information is recorded in each country's balance sheet? In the United States, a liability: American statisticians see that foreigners hold US equities. In Switzerland, nothing at all, and for a reason: the Swiss statisticians see some Google stock deposited in a Swiss bank, but they see that the stock belongs to a UK resident—and so they are neither assets nor liabilities for Switzerland. In the United Kingdom, nothing is registered, either, but wrongly this time: the Office for National Statistics should record an asset for the United Kingdom, but it can't, because it has no way of knowing that the British person has Google stock in her Geneva account.
>
> As we can see, an anomaly arises—more liabilities than assets will tend to be recorded on a global level. And, in fact, for as far back as statistics go, there is a "hole": if we look at the world balance sheet, more financial securities are recorded as liabilities than as assets, as if planet Earth were in part held by Mars.

The secrecy surrounding tax havens like Switzerland, makes it difficult to ascertain who owns the hidden wealth, and thus which individuals are evading taxes, and by how much. Estimates of tax evasion have typically been based on random tax audits. But these audits include very few individuals at the very top of the wealth and income distribution, and they fail to detect evasion involving shell companies and hidden accounts. This also means that measures of wealth inequality that are based on tax data alone will grossly underestimate the actual amount of wealth at the top of the pyramid.

Research by Alstadsæter et al. (2017), analyzes data made available by two massive leaks from offshore financial institutions. The first data were obtained in 2007 from the internal records of HSBC Private Bank. Known as "Swiss Leaks", they were released in 2015 by the International Consortium of Investigative Journalists (ICIJ). One leak included the names of the owners of the wealth the bank managed, even when the ownership was concealed through a network of shell companies in offshore tax havens. The other leak, knows as "The Panama Papers", was released in 2016 by the ICIJ. It contained the names and addresses of the owners of shell companies created by the Panamanian firm Mossack Fonseca. It confirmed that the use of tax havens rises steeply with wealth. Thirdly, an additional source of information comes from households who have previously disclosed their hidden wealth voluntarily in exchange for reduced penalties due to tax amnesties in Norway and Sweden.

Combining information from these sources with administrative income and wealth records in Norway, Sweden, and Denmark, the researchers observe a sharp upward gradient in tax evasion by wealth groups. The average evasion of taxes as a percent of taxes owed is estimated around 3 percent. Households in the top 0.01 percent, however, a group of households each with more than $40 million in net wealth, evades about 30 percent of its personal income and wealth taxes (Alstadsæter et al. 2017: 2). The propensity to hide wealth also seems to rise sharply with wealth. The top 0.01 percent of Norwegian and Swedish households, each with more than $40 million in net wealth, is found to be 250 times more likely than average to hide their assets. This group owns about 50 percent of all wealth held offshore, hiding about 25 percent of their true wealth from the authorities. The authors point out (Alstadsæter et al. 2017: 3–4):

> Our results highlight the need to move beyond tax records to capture the income and wealth of the very rich, even in countries where tax compliance is generally high. They also suggest that tax data may significantly underestimate the rise of wealth concentration over the last four decades, as the world was less globalized in the 1970s, it was harder to move assets across borders, and offshore tax havens played a less important role. Because most

Latin American, and many Asian and European economies own much more wealth offshore than Norway, the results found in Scandinavia are likely to be a lower bound for most of the world's countries.

It is important to remember that simply owning a bank account in places like Switzerland is not a crime per se: but not reporting it to the tax authorities is. The study shows that about 95 percent of the Norwegian and Danish individuals identified as owning an account in HSBC Switzerland, had not reported it, allowing the researchers to identify them as tax evaders.

Alstadsæter et al.'s (2017) work shows that among Scandinavians with bank accounts in Switzerland, 95 percent failed to provide information about these to the Inland Revenue Service. The study also shows that the hidden foreigners are strongly concentrated in the approximately 1100 richest families in Scandinavia, which make up about 0.01 percent of the population. The findings do not support the hypothesis that the most resourceful among us are the most honorable. Nor do they find support for the claim that many own a bank account in Switzerland for legitimate reasons. On the contrary, the findings indicate that most people who choose to put their money into a tax haven do it as financial criminals (Jacobsen and Coll 2017).

ABUSE OF MACROECONOMIC ESTIMATES

Given the uncertainty in all macroeconomic estimates of crime—be it white-collar crime, tax evasion, or social security fraud—it is extremely important to be cautious in the application of such numbers in political and management arguments. While it may be easy for journalists, politicians, law enforcement, and others to grab a large number and use it for their own agenda and in their own context, abuse of numbers with an intentional purpose is very unethical. Therefore, we must caution every reader not to jump on a bandwagon that the magnitude of white-collar crime is 12 billion NOK in Norway and thus must be billions of dollars in the United States ($96 billion) by assuming the same occurrence rate in a much larger population.

An example can be drawn from the Norwegian daily business newspaper *Dagens Næringsliv* in which it was claimed that attorneys from global auditing firm PwC abused social security estimates from NAV, which we discussed earlier in this book, to emphasize that employers should not believe employees who claim they are sick. The newspaper's front page was covered with the following statement: "Ask employers to intervene against cheating with sickness reports", by PwC lawyers Ida Solberg Henning and Lene Sakariassen (Kaspersen 2017: 22–23):

> Misuse of the sickness benefit scheme costs two to three billion a year. This is something employers can and should do something about, says PwC lawyers.
>
> Between six and eight percent of the sickness payout is probably not enough justified or direct abuse of the sickness benefit scheme, according to a report Proba Research prepared on behalf of the Ministry of Labor. It indicates between 2.2 and 2.9 billion annual costs, based on what is granted for sickness benefit over the state budget for 2017.
>
> "If the employer has clear indications that an employee is not ill, he has the opportunity to contest the sickness report, i.e. refusing to pay for the first 16 sick days", says lawyer Ida Solberg Henning, who works with labor law at the law firm PwC.
>
> The employer generally has a duty to pay sickness benefits for the first 16 calendar days a worker is ill. After that, Nav assumes responsibility.
>
> To be entitled to sickness benefit, you must be unemployed because of a disability that is clearly due to your own illness or injury. Henning and colleague Lene Sakariassen emphasize that most of the sickness reports are legitimate, but in some cases it is clear that the conditions for sickness benefits are not met.
>
> "For example, if a worker becomes ill-reported when he or she has been refused leave for vacation, there is a conflict at work, or if the employee is at risk of termination", Henning says.
>
> The lawyers emphasize that there is a risk associated with such a process. Should the disputes prove to be based on a wrong basis, this could have consequences for the company – both economically and for the internal working environment.
>
> That's why there are many employers who are struggling to address problems with sickness and sick leave.
>
> "But to contest sickness reports that are strongly suspected to be incorrect is to take on corporate social responsibility", claim the PwC attorneys.
>
> A week's sick leave costs an average Norwegian employer around 15,000 kroner, which is a number from Sintef. In addition to the fact that the employer has to pay sickness benefits, costs related to production losses, any expenses for a replacement and overtime may occur.
>
> "Employers' expenses related to the sick leave absence period which are not sufficiently justified or direct abuse of the sickness benefit scheme amount to several hundred million kroner a year. Costs related to sickness

absence extending beyond the employer's period come in addition", summarizes Ida Solberg Henning.

In a report prepared by Oxford Research, it appears that the Appeals Committee for Social Security in the Employer's Period had 86 such cases about the employee's incapacity for work in the years 2014–2015. In two out of three cases, the employer won the case.

"Then it's natural to think that employers have helped to prevent abuse of the sickness benefit scheme," PwC lawyers point out.

Fortunately, some estimates are better founded than others. The research by Alstadsæter et al. (2017) is one such example (Jacobsen and Coll 2017: 28):

Most previous studies on individuals' tax evasion in tax havens have either had to make use of estimates, or highly aggregated data. Here, however, the researchers have used unique data sets from data leakages SwissLeaks and Panama Papers. This is information obtained directly from banks and law firms in tax havens, which they have been able to match with data from the Scandinavian tax authorities.

REFERENCES

Alstadsæter, A., Johannesen, N., & Zucman, G. (2017). *Tax Evasion and Inequality* (Working Paper). Paper and Data Appendix available at: http://gabriel-zucman.eu

Altindag, D. T. (2012). Crime and Unemployment: Evidence from Europe. *International Review of Law and Economics, 32*, 145–157.

Andersen, J. J., Johannesen, N., Lassen, D. D., & Paltseva, E. (2017). Petro Rents, Political Institutions, and Hidden Wealth: Evidence from Offshore Bank Accounts. Journal of the European Economic Association, Volume 15, Issue 4, 1 August 2017, Pages 818–860, https://doi.org/10.1093/jeea/jvw019

Breusch, T. (2005). *Estimating the Underground Economy Using MIMIC Models*. Paper provided by EconWPA in its series Econometrics with number 0507003. http://econwpa.repec.org/eps/em/papers/0507/0507003.pdf

Cebula, R. J. (2012). Revisiting Property Crime and Economic Conditions: An Exploratory Study to Identify Predictive Indicators Beyond Unemployment Rates – Comment. *The Social Science Journal, 49*, 314–316.

Ceccato, V., & Benson, M. L. (2016). Tax Evasion in Sweden 2002–2013: Interpreting Changes in the Rot/Rut Deduction System and Predicting Future Trends. *Crime, Law and Social Change, 66*, 217–232.

Edelbacher, M., Dobovsek, B., & Kratcoski, P. C. (2016). The Relationship of the Informal Economy to Corruption, Fraud, and Organized Crime. In M. Edelbacher, P. C. Kratcoski, & B. Dobovsek (Eds.), *Corruption, Fraud, Organized Crime, and the Shadow Economy*. Boca Raton: CRC Press, Taylor & Francis.

Evans, M. (2016). Social Capital and the Shadow Economy. *Journal of Economic Issues*, *L*(1), 43–58.

Hegnar, T. (2017, June 9, Friday). *De superrike og skatt* [The Super-Rich and Tax]. Daily Norwegian financial newspaper *Finansavisen*, p. 2.

Hendriyetty, N., & Grewal, B. S. (2017). Macroeconomics of Money Laundering: Effects and Measurements. *Journal of Financial Crime*, *24*(1), 65–81.

Henry, J. (2012). *The Price of Offshore Revisited. New Estimates for "Missing" Global Private Wealth, Income, Inequality, and Lost Taxes*. Tax Justice Network.

Imamoglu, H. (2016). Re-estimation of the Size of Underground Economy in European Countries: MIMIC Approach. *International Journal of Economic Perspectives*, *10*(1), 171–193.

Jacobsen, S. K., & Coll, I. A. E. (2017, June 10, Saturday). *Galskap å legge ned Økokrim* [Madness to Close Down Økokrim (Norwegian National Authority for Investigation and Prosecution of Economic and Environmental Crime)]. Daily Norwegian Business Newspaper *Dagens Næringsliv*, p. 28.

Kaspersen, L. (2017). Ber sjefen gripe inn mot juks med sykemeldinger. *Dagens Næringsliv*, mandag 12. januar, side 22–23.

Petersen, H. G., Thiessen, U., & Wohlleben, P. (2010). Shadow Economy, Tax Evasion, and Transfer Fraud – Definition, Measurement, and Data Problems. *International Economic Journal*, *24*(4), 421–441.

Samfunnsøkonomisk analyse. (2017). *Analyse av former, omfang og utvikling av arbeidsmarkedskriminalitet* [Analysis of the Forms, Scope and Development of Labor Market Crime]. Oslo: Samfunnsøkonomisk analyse. www.samfunnsokonomisk-analyse.no

Schneider, F., & Williams, C. C. (2013). *The Shadow Economy*. London: The Institute of Economic Affairs.

Schneider, F., Buehn, A., & Montenegro, C. E. (2010). *Shadow Economies All over the World: New Estimates for 162 Countries from 1999 to 2007*. The World Bank, Development Research Group, Poverty and Inequality Team. www.gfintegrity.org.

Yearwood, D. L., & Koinis, G. (2011). Revisiting Property Crime and Economic Conditions: An Exploratory Study to Identify Predictive Indicators Beyond Unemployment Rates. *The Social Science Journal*, *48*, 145–158.

Zucman, G. (2015). *The Hidden Wealth of Nations. The Scourge of Tax Havens*. The University of Chicago Press. http://gabriel-zucman.eu/hidden-wealth/

Open Access This chapter is licensed under the terms of the Creative Commons Attribution 4.0 International License (http://creativecommons.org/licenses/by/4.0/), which permits use, sharing, adaptation, distribution and reproduction in any medium or format, as long as you give appropriate credit to the original author(s) and the source, provide a link to the Creative Commons license and indicate if changes were made.

The images or other third party material in this chapter are included in the chapter's Creative Commons license, unless indicated otherwise in a credit line to the material. If material is not included in the chapter's Creative Commons license and your intended use is not permitted by statutory regulation or exceeds the permitted use, you will need to obtain permission directly from the copyright holder.

CHAPTER 10

White-Collar Crime Detection

Abstract In Norway, 405 white-collar offenders were convicted and imprisoned between 2009 and 2016. Journalists detected 25 percent of these criminals, followed by crime victims, bankruptcy attorneys, internal auditors, tax authority clerks, bank employees, external auditors, and police officers. Many of these detections were based on whistleblowing to external journalists, internal auditors, and others. The sum of money involved in crime is significantly larger in cases detected by journalists. Only 5 percent of the criminals in our sample were detected by auditors. Signal detection theory may shed some light on why some actors discover and disclose more white-collar crime than others. It holds that the detection of a stimulus depends on both the intensity of the stimulus and the physical and psychological state of the individual.

Keywords Auditor detection • Crime detection source • External auditor • Internal auditor • Journalist detection • Media coverage • Screening theory • Signal alertness • Signal detection theory • Whistleblower

This book is concerned with the magnitude of white-collar crime. We define convicted white-collar criminals as the tip of an iceberg. Based on expert elicitation, we have estimated the tip to be only 9.2 percent of the total iceberg, since 1.1 billion NOK are detected annually, while the estimated magnitude is 11.9 billion NOK annually.

White-Collar Versus Social Security

We contrast white-collar crime with social security fraud on the spectrum of financial crime. We argue that while social security fraud is committed by people with small and limited resources, white-collar crime is committed by people with large and almost unlimited resources. Based on studies by Proba (2011, 2013), the tip of the total iceberg for social security fraud is estimated at 3.1 percent, since 0.3 billion NOK are detected annually, while the estimated magnitude is 9.8 billion NOK annually.

A number of perspectives can be applied when discussing white-collar crime and social security fraud:

- Crime at the top in private businesses, political bodies, and government agencies can be a greater problem in society than most have thought. The head of the Norwegian police unit for investigating economic crime believes that three out of four economic criminals probably go free, and that the chance of being caught should be larger than one to four. Estimates in this book suggest that the situation is much worse.
- The tip of the white-collar crime iceberg represents crime at a cost of more than 1 billion Norwegian kroner every year, for which white-collar offenders are convicted and imprisoned. We used a panel of 15 experts to estimate the real scale of white-collar crime in Norway. The overall estimate is more than ten times larger than what is visible in court verdicts: 12 billion NOK annually.
- While very many white-collar criminals go free, the Norwegian media, politicians, and authorities direct their efforts to social security fraud. The proportion of police reports from NAV (the Norwegian labor and welfare service/Norwegian social security authority) not being pursued through the courts dropped from 25 percent in 2011 to 15 percent in 2015 (i.e., there was an increase in the percentage prosecuted over this period). We question whether Norwegian society prioritizes the fight against white-collar crime strenuously enough.
- The media and the government are doing a lot to emphasize social security fraud as a significant and major problem in society. White-collar crime, on the other hand, is referred to as individual cases, not as a fundamental problem in society. Our estimate suggests that white-collar crime costs society more than social security fraud and,

in that sense, is a larger problem and more of a threat to a modern democratic society such as Norway.
- It is in our view not objectively justified—or in the interests of society—for the government and media to punch harder and more strenouously at welfare fraud than on elite offences.
- Regarding the rule of law, it is particularly unfortunate if discrimination within law enforcement arises because it is more natural for humans within the managing elite to perceive law violations by those "down there" (the social security fraudsters) as a more fundamental problem in society than law violations by those "up there" (white-collar offenders) who themselves belong to the elite.

The share of reports from NAV dismissed by the police reduced from 24 percent in 2011 to 15 percent in 2015. And almost every court case against those accused of welfare fraud in 2015 found the defendant guilty (97 percent of cases). This means that a very large proportion of people being accused of committing welfare fraud end up being sentenced. But what does this tell us about the probability of actually being caught?

We know that all the cases NAV reports to the police each year amount to as little as 0.15 percent of total welfare payments (about 300 million NOK in 2015). Comparing this observed amount with the expert assessment of welfare fraud on a scale of about 5 percent of total payments each year (10 billion NOK in 2015), leaves us with two possible explanations.

For the numbers to add up, NAV must have a fraud detection rate of about 3 percent (0.15 out of 5). (It seems unlikely that the detection rate in reality is even lower than this, but it cannot be ruled out.) Alternatively, if NAV's detection rate in reality is higher than 3 percent, then the established estimate of 5 percent welfare fraud has to be deemed unreasonably large.

NAV's own employees assess that they detect about 11 percent of all fraud being committed each year. If that were the case, we would be looking at fraud amounting to about 1.4 percent (0.15/0.11) of total payments each year, or about 3 billion NOK in 2015.

Unlike the United States, Norway has no large African-American or Spanish-speaking minority. Unlike the UK, Norway has no large minority from former colonies. Minorities in Norway have emerged recently as a consequence of labor migration and refugee routes. As in most other countries, minorities are overrepresented in welfare programs administered by NAV in Norway and as experienced by front-line workers at NAV (Terum et al. 2017: 4):

> North Africans (particularly Somalis) constitute the largest minority group on social assistance. Norwegian ethnographic studies indicate that front-line workers experience Somalian men to be particularly demanding. Somalian recipients have also reported being treated arbitrarily and disrespectfully and experiencing personally invasive behavior by front-line workers.

Terum et al. (2017) studied discrimination in the implementation of social programs administered by NAV. The researchers expected to find similar discrimination in Norway towards claimants with North African names, as other researchers have found regarding Spanish and African-American names in the United States. However, both demographical and cultural differences exist between the welfare systems of the United States, the UK, and Norway, which probably create dissimilar tendencies. Norwegian welfare programs are considered generous and reach a larger proportion of the population.

In particular, Terum et al. (2017: 5) studied potential discrimination in the qualification program in Norway, which is a program established as the main policy instrument to fight poverty and social exclusion:

> The aim of the program is to improve the labor market attachment of claimants who have complex problems and cannot immediately be integrated into the labor market but, nonetheless, are deemed capable of working. The program targets individuals who are long-term recipients of social assistance. Unlike social assistance, the qualification program is not only a benefit scheme but also a full-time activation program, where claimants are referred to as participants. Each participant in the program has a right to an individually designed weekly plan that involves 37.5 hours of extensive training, counseling and related activities geared towards increasing their opportunities of finding ordinary work.

Terum et al. (2017) conducted an experiment involving 470 Norwegian front-line workers to investigate whether their decisions to sanction noncompliance of activation requirements varied with the ethnicity of the welfare claimant. The study shows that front-line workers did not sanction claimants with a North African name more often than claimants with a native Norwegian name.

Table 10.1 Detection of white-collar crime

Rank	Crime detection source	Criminals	Fraction (%)
1	Journalists investigating tips from readers	101	25
2	Crime victims suffering financial loss	52	13
3	Bankruptcy attorneys identifying misconduct	45	11
4	Internal auditors controlling transactions	45	11
5	Tax authority clerks carrying out controls	25	6
6	Bank employees controlling accounts	18	4
7	External auditors controlling clients	18	4
8	Police officers investigating financial crime	9	2
9	Stock exchange clerks controlling transactions	4	1
10	Other knowledge workers as detection sources	88	23
	Total	**405**	**100**

CRIME SIGNAL DETECTION

In Norway, 405 white-collar offenders were convicted and imprisoned between 2009 and 2016. Table 10.1 lists how these criminals were detected. We find journalists occupy the top crime detection source position, followed by crime victims, bankruptcy attorneys, internal auditors, tax authority clerks, bank employees, external auditors, and police officers. Many of these detections were based on whistleblowing to external journalists, internal auditors, and others.

SOURCES OF CRIME DETECTION

A comparison of the white-collar crime cases detected by journalists, with those detected by others, is presented in Table 10.2. Some interesting differences are statistically significant. First, the sum of money involved in crime is significantly larger in cases detected by journalists. The average amount for journalist-detected criminals is 110 million NOK (approximately $14 million). The statistical analysis in Table 10.2 and the following tables was implemented with a sample size of 369 convicted white-collar criminals.

Strangely, criminals detected by journalists are registered with a lower income, less tax, and fewer assets than white-collar criminals detected by others. Not so strange, however, is that the number of people involved in criminal activity is larger in cases detected by journalists. External detection is probably easier when more criminals are involved in the offense.

Table 10.2 Comparison of journalist and non-journalist detected white-collar criminals

Total 369 white-collar criminals	97 detected by journalists	272 detected by others	T-statistic difference	Significance of t-statistic
Age convicted	48 years	48 years	−0.512	0.609
Age at time of crime	43 years	44 years	−0.893	0.372
Years in prison	2.5 years	2.2 years	1.659	0.098
Crime amount	110m NOK	26m NOK	4.783	0.000
Personal income	260,000 NOK	429,000 NOK	−2.058	0.040
Personal tax	113,000 NOK	201,000 NOK	−2.185	0.030
Personal wealth	1.6m NOK	3.2m NOK	−1.050	0.294
Involved persons	5.0 persons	2.8 persons	8.186	0.000
Business revenue	234m NOK	214m NOK	0.381	0.704
Business employees	136 persons	132 persons	0.094	0.925

Some of the characteristics are not significantly different. For example, criminals detected by journalists have the same age as criminals detected by others. Likewise, criminals detected by journalists are associated with organizations of about the same size as criminals detected by others.

When we compare financial crime categories committed by white-collar criminals, in terms of detection, results indicate that journalists tend to detect fraud to a great extent, but in less of the other categories, as shown in Table 10.3.

Since a substantial fraction of white-collar criminals are detected by journalists, and very few are detected by traditional law enforcement agencies, there might be lessons to be learned from media working procedures. Journalists review information and information sources in established and developing networks of individuals located in key areas of the economy. Journalists study accounting reports and other information, and receive documents from their network of sources. They interview attorneys, competitors, the police, and authorities. They set a case aside for weeks and months until new information emerges. In the meantime, they keep the information top secret, until publication for the first time.

Investigative journalists tend to develop hypotheses about phenomena and causality. They are very different from reporting journalists who only tend to relate what they have heard or seen. Investigative journalists

Table 10.3 Financial crime categories by detection sources

Crime category	Total detected in each crime category	Journalist detection in each category	Journalist detection fraction (%)
Fraud	160	52	33
Theft	17	2	12
Manipulation	127	28	22
Corruption	65	13	20
Total	369	95	26

develop an idea via a study of potential offenders and their victims. They apply systematic analysis and generally treat their sources with care and professional concern.

In most criminal areas, it is expected that a combination of victim and police is the main source of criminal detection. After crime victims suffer an injury or a loss, they tend to report the incident to the police who investigate and hopefully find the offender(s). In cases of financial crime by white-collar criminals, it is often quite different. A victim is frequently not aware of the injury or loss. For example, accounting fraud resulting in tax evasion is not a harm or damage perceived by tax authorities.

A number of angles can be explored in the process of white-collar crime detection within the news media. In addition, we have the news media (newspapers and online media) that specialize and focus on financial information of all sorts, and report on this regularly. For these media, the sources of information can be traditional, for example, tip-offs, company reports, stock-exchange information, and press conferences, as well as other sources. For regular news media spread out over the country, the situation can be quite different. The detection of white-collar crime can arise from a tip-off from a whistleblower or as official information if the police or an economic crime prosecutor performs a search locally. Whistleblowers in many cases alert journalists to serious crime and are sometimes the true detectors, not the journalists or media.

Additionally, the way the news is treated in the news media is dependent on many variables that occur at the same time: Do the media have the right journalists in place at the time? Do they have an interest in the matter? Do they know anything or anyone related to this? There will also be a resource balance taking place. The resource perspective in leading media houses is concerned with knowledge management.

Not many news media outside of the larger ones will be able to allocate journalists to work on an investigative white-collar crime for months. In the cases where they have done this, editors seems to be uncertain as to whether this allocation of resources was worthwhile relative to the size and the complexity of the case. For a common, non-specialist news media, there will always be a balance between resources and the newsworthiness of the matter at hand. If a major white-collar crime story had emerged in Norway in the weeks after the July 22 terrorist attacks in 2011, it is unlikely that the story would have attracted much attention in the general public press.

The general news media have a constant incoming flow of news on hand, and there is an ongoing daily prioritization of what is important and what should be published. For all news items there are some general rules of journalism that come into play: Is the item important to many people? Is it really news? Is it possible to get reliable information on this? Is it possible to approach the right people with the right questions? Can both parties in a conflict be approached? And in addition to these questions, there will be a question as to whether the news organization at this point in time has the resources to deal with the item. If the journalist knowledgeable about economic matters is on holiday, it is doubtful whether the news media organization will come back to the item at a later date. That will depend on the development and the newsworthiness of the item at the second point in time. If the news organization is the first to report on a crime and it is regarded as "hot", it will probably do whatever possible to handle the matter at hand, knowing that other media, and especially online media, can report on the same matter and as such "steal" the story. There is always internal pride in a news organization when it can report on a matter of significant interest, and be cited by other news organizations.

The organizational culture also has an influence on white-collar crime detection among journalists. If you have journalists that are driven to win investigative journalism prizes (e.g., SKUP in Norway), there is a higher possibility that such stories will be published. But this will differ greatly among news organizations. Øvrebø (2004) showed in a study of the Norwegian newspaper *Dagsavisen* that after a change of editor-in-chief in 2001, the news profile and priorities of the newspaper changed according to the principles laid down by the new editor when she took up her position. It can be argued that an editor's personal preferences can influence the news priorities of a newspaper, and this relates to all types of editorial material, whether it is general, sports, culture, or financial news.

For a general news organization, white-collar crime is not a big story in itself unless it has repercussions for well-known people locally or if something happens to the organization where the crime has taken place. Nationally, it can be a big story if the person is well-known or if the crime in itself is of an unusual nature. If a main employer locally has to file for bankruptcy because of a white-collar crime, then the story is more than just another white-collar crime case since it has wider consequences that turn the world upside down for ordinary people in this local area. Then the white-collar crime story will take the form of another typical, important, news story and be followed and treated as such, and the white-collar crime element will be mixed with other elements and consequential stories, building on the starting point as a white-collar crime story. Campbell (1997) studied the journalistic process of environmental news in Scotland, and addressed the information sources which are used in the news process. The study showed the preference for human sources as opposed to library-based information and discussed the influence of pragmatic constraints like time and space on the production of news. It can be argued that this process is similar to the news-gathering process for white collar crime.

The argument of white-collar crime detection among journalists seems to be related to the story's importance in itself and, as such, it will be treated as just another crime or news story and have the same internal process. For smaller news organizations without journalistic specialization in financial matters, the white-collar crime story will be treated according to the news prioritizing structure of that particular organization. For larger news organizations that typically have separate sections for financial and economic news, the story will be treated within the prioritizing of that particular section. And if the story is big enough in total it will be moved from the particular finance or economics section into the general news section of the organization. The higher the profile of those involved, the more likely it is that the story will have a more centralized coverage; it will be moved into what is often the first section of the newspaper or the prioritized areas of a website's front page.

The first four of the 10 detector categories in Table 10.1 made up 60% of the total crime detecting sources and out of these the first two—journalists investigating tips from readers and crime victims suffering loss— made up 38%. It can be argued that these two categories are more susceptible to journalistic interest than the others, simply because it is easier to construct news stories based on these journalistic angles. Themes like manipulation and corruption are much more difficult to make into a story that is interesting for the readers simply because it is more complex and difficult to describe these matters in layman's terms. A tip from readers that is given to a news medium is, most of the time, accompanied by a subjective story from the person giving the tip that in turn gives the journalist clues to work with and discuss internally in order to assign the right news priority and angle. This is also supported by the breakdown in Table 10.3 showing that fraud is the category having the highest percentage of journalistic detection.

White-collar crime detection and follow up seems to be related to a number of simultaneous journalistic procedures and cultural elements. For specialized publications in the financial information area, the white-collar crime news arena is closer at hand and the organization will typically be able to delve deeper into the matter. If white-collar crime is detected by general or local news organizations, the procedure involved will more often take the form of a general news story with the resource balance that follows from that. It can also be shown that white-collar crime is more often detected by journalists if it is based on a tip from readers or if it is reported as fraud. Underlying all this are the internal news preferences and editorial guidance that are part of the policies of the news medium.

Finally, the most obvious reason for the high detection fraction by journalists is the fact that one of the criteria for our sample is newspaper coverage of the case. Naturally, this will lead to a bias towards journalist detection.

Auditing Role in Crime Detection

The role of auditing in the detection of white-collar crime is an interesting topic, as it is not obvious that auditors are able to detect crime. This might have to do with the responsibilities of auditing functions as well as procedures and practices followed by auditors in their work. For example, Beasley (2003) is concerned with the fact that auditors seem to struggle with reducing occurrences of material misstatements due to fraud, even in the light of new auditing standards. The focus of new standards remains on fraudulent activities that lead to intentional material misstatements due to fraud, and it expands the guidance and procedures to be performed in every audit. The expanded guidance might hopefully lead to improvements in auditor detection of material misstatements due to fraud, by strengthening the auditor's responses to identified high fraud risks.

One of the surprising results of this research is the lack of crime detection by auditors: Only 18 (4 percent) of the 405 criminals in our sample were detected by auditors. Moyes and Baker (2003) asked external, internal, and governmental auditors to evaluate the effectiveness of various standard audit procedures in detecting fraud. Although external and internal auditors differed in the types of audit procedures they recommended, the authors conclude that "the audit procedures judged more effective in detecting fraud were those which provided evidence about the existence of internal controls and those which evaluated the strength of internal controls", and that "strategic use of standard audit procedures may help auditors fulfill their responsibilities under SAS No. 99" (Moyes and Baker 2003: 199). Furthermore, "the results of this study indicate that fraud detection might be improved through the strategic use of standard audit procedures earlier in the audit examination....If these audit procedures were applied during the preliminary stages of the audit, they would be more likely to indicate the potential existence of fraud, in which case the auditor would have more time to revise the audit plan and conduct other necessary investigations" (Moyes and Baker 2003: 216).

Similarly, Albrecht et al. (2001) reviewed fraud detection aspects of current auditing standards and the empirical and other research that has been conducted on fraud detection. They concluded that "even though the red flag approach to detecting fraud has been endorsed by policy makers and written about widely by researchers, there is little empirical evidence that shows the red flag approach is an effective way to detect fraud, especially for fraud that has yet to be discovered" (Albrecht et al. 2001: 4). Their research review on the subject reveals that one of the major conclusions drawn from previous studies included the fact that only 18–20% of frauds appear to be detected by internal and external auditors, and further that only about half of the perpetrators of frauds detected are duly prosecuted. The article also calls for further fraud detection research. These detection rates are loosely corroborated by Silverstone and Sheetz (2003), who estimate that approximately 12 percent of initial fraud detection is through external audit, and approximately 19 percent arises from internal audit. (Both of these estimations apply to the American context.)

An article dealing with the responsibilities for prevention and detection of white-collar crime refers to a study undertaken to map how members of the accounting profession viewed the changing role of the external auditor following the introduction of SAS No. 82 (Farrell and Healy 2000: 25):

Most of those answering the questionnaire disagreed that they should be responsible for searching for fraud....Clearly, this notion concerning the auditor's responsibility is not widely held by the public at large....The general public and Congress certainly sided against the CPAs and was the reason for this legislation.

As to the question of whether certified public accountants (CPAs) should act as police or detectives when performing an audit, the response was a resounding no (Farrell and Healy 2000: 25):

This may also indicate that changes brought about with the implementation of the SAS No. 82 requiring a *policing component* clearly require added responsibility and may necessitate additional training and changes to job description requirements. Again, although the general public may believe policing is within the auditors' duties, even SAS No. 82 does not require this.

Similarly, an investigation into fraud prevention and detection in the United States uncovered that the majority of CPAs that responded to the study believed the external auditor's responsibility for fraud detection extends only to assessing the probability of fraud and planning the audit accordingly. They ranked internal auditors as the group most effective in detecting fraud, followed by fraud examiners and client management.

Jones (2004: 12–13) presents a slightly more balanced view on the auditor's role in crime detection:

A persistent debate has dogged relationships between auditors and managers. This debate revolves around the precise roles and duties of each party in relation to fraud and corruption, and particularly who should take responsibility for investigation. Current legal and professional precedents leave little doubt that management bears the main responsibility for ensuring that reasonable measures are taken to prevent fraud and corruption. In any event it is common practice for managers to request assistance and advice from auditors upon suspicion or discovery of fraud. The final responsibility must lie with managers unless the auditor has given specific assurance regarding particular controls or the absence of error or fraud.

In a study in Norway, researchers found that 11 percent of cases of white-collar crime were detected by auditing functions. This is lower than the 4 percent (according to our sample) reported above, and also significantly lower than the results presented by Albrecht et al. (2001), Moyes and Baker (2003), and Silverstone and Sheetz (2003). The figures of 4 percent and 11 percent in Norway indicate that Norwegian auditing has an even less pronounced role in the detection of white-collar crime than the measurements performed in the United States, for example.

Iver and Samociuk (2006) argue that fraud risks need to be recorded, monitored, and reported. Such recording includes the nature of each risk, its likelihood and consequences, the current and suggested controls, and the owner of the risk for follow-up action.

Within the extant accounting and auditing research, a great deal of attention is devoted to how the external auditor is a primary figure in detecting irregularities and corruption, and government and standard setters also stress the importance of the responsibilities of the auditing community in this respect. However, there seems to be limited faith and responsibility in the auditing function among some in this specific purpose: Only in very few cases does auditing in some form seem to be responsible for the detection, unraveling, and exposure of the offence. This opinion is backed up by the work of Drage and Olstad (2008), who analyzed the role of the auditing function in relation to both preventing and detecting white-collar crime. Although their study included a look at the perceived preventative power of the auditing function as well as actual detection of criminal offences, their findings were consistent with the abovementioned hypothesis: Many of their interviewees were skeptical regarding the auditing function having a central role in the detection of white-collar crime.

Olsen (2007) reminds us that the auditing standards that external auditors must act in compliance with also require them to uncover irregularities should they be present. However, the primary concern of the external auditor is to reduce the auditing risk (i.e., the risk that the financial statements may still contain material misstatements even after the auditor has given a positive auditor report), not the risk of irregularities. In spite of external auditors rarely being credited for the detection of financial crime, Olsen (2007) still believes that the auditing function contributes significantly to the prevention of such crime by reducing temptations and opportunities, thus corroborating the findings of Drage and Olstad (2008) on prevention.

Rendal and Westerby (2010) examined Norwegian auditors' expectations regarding their own abilities in detecting and preventing irregularities and compared these with the expectations other users of financial information have of this same issue. Their findings indicate certain gaps in terms of how the auditor is expected to perform. Auditors themselves answer that they sometimes do not act in accordance with laws and regulations, and both auditors and users of financial information feel that the auditing function should include more than what is required today through standards and regulations, for example, pertaining to companies' internal guidelines. They also uncover unrealistic expectations regarding the extent to which the auditing function is capable of uncovering irregularities. They conclude that, to a certain extent, auditors are too reserved and aloof when it comes to their responsibilities in the prevention and detection of irregularities, and call for improvements.

Crime Signal Detection Theory

In the sample of 405 white-collar crime convicts in Norway, we identified the sources of detection as follows—journalists 25%, victims 13%, bankruptcy auditors 11%, internal auditors 11%, internal revenue employees at the Norwegian Tax Administration 6%, bank clerks 4%, external auditors 4%, police officers 2%, stock exchange employees 1%, and others 23% (see Table 10.1). Crime signal detection theory can shed light on why many white-collar crimes are detected by journalists, and relatively few are detected by internal revenue employees and others further down the list.

Signal detection theory may shed some light on why some actors discover and disclose more white-collar crime than others. Signal detection theory holds that the detection of a stimulus depends on both the intensity of the stimulus and the physical and psychological state of the individual. A detector's ability or likelihood to detect some stimulus is affected by the intensity of the stimulus (e.g., how loud a whistleblower is) and the detector's physical and psychological state (e.g., how alert hoe or she is). Perceptual sensitivity depends upon the perceptual ability of the observer to detect a signal or target or to discriminate signal from non-signal events (Szalma and Hancock 2013).

Furthermore, those detecting may have varying abilities to discern between information-bearing recognition (called pattern) and random patterns that distract from information (called noise).

Under signal detection theory, some researchers found that people more frequently and incorrectly identify negative task-related words as originally having been presented than positive words, even when they were not present. Liu et al. (2014) found that people have lax decision criteria for negative words. In a different study, Huff and Bodner (2013) applied the signal detection approach to determine if changes in correct and false recognition following item-specific versus relational encoding were driven by a decrease in the encoding of memory information or by an increase in monitoring at test.

According to the theory, there are a number of determinants of how a person will detect a signal. In addition to signal intensity, signal alertness, and pattern recognition, there are other factors such as personal competence (including knowledge, skills, and attitude), experience, and expectations. These factors determine the threshold level. Low signal intensity, low signal alertness, and limited pattern recognition, combined with low competence, lack of experience, and lack of expectations will lead to a high threshold level, meaning that the individual will not detect white-collar crime.

The competence of private investigators is a concern. For several decades, they have strived to achieve professional status, arguing that their work is a skilled activity requiring long and in-depth training. Private policing, which is not regulated by statue in countries such as the UK, the United States, or Norway, directly challenges this premise. People are not required to undergo any form of training in order to set up as private investigators.

Signal detection theory implies that people make decisions under conditions of uncertainty. The theory assumes that the decision-maker is not a passive recipient of information, but an active decision-maker who makes difficult perceptual judgments under conditions of uncertainty. Whether a stimulus is present or absent, whether a stimulus is perceived or not perceived, whether a perceived stimulus is ignored or not, will influence the decision in terms of detecting or not detecting white-collar crime.

Gomulya and Mishina (2017: 557) introduce the term signal susceptibility due to the fact that signals may be differently susceptible to potential errors and manipulation:

> This could be due to a variety of possible reasons, including whether the signal is self- or other-reported, whether it is verifiable, or whether it is a "stock" or a "flow" signal. Self-reported signals should on average be more susceptible to manipulations by the focal signaler (i.e., the one who can benefit from a positive signal) compared to signals reported by third parties.

Given this definition, signal susceptibility can be included as an aspect of signal intensity, where signal intensity deteriorates on suspicion of errors and manipulation increases. Similarly, noise in general will reduce signal intensity. Gomulya and Mishina (2017: 555) distinguish between two sources of noise during signaling—noise from the signal itself and noise from the behavior of the signaler.

Another term introduced by Gomulya and Mishina (2017: 55) is signal reliance, where reliance on different types of signals is based on the credibility of the signaler, and "thus a similar signal is likely to have different effects for credible versus less credible" signalers. Given this perspective, signal reliance can be included as an aspect of signal alertness, where less credible signalers display lower alertness to the signal.

Gomulya and Mishina (2017) discuss pattern recognition in terms of screening theory where the recipient prioritizes among possible types of signals. The focus is on how recipients place differential value on signals that may come from different senders, such as documents, accounts, and individuals. Screening theory posits that recipients screen by focusing on signals that they believe are highly correlated with unobservable characteristics of interest.

Signal detection theory characterizes the activity of an individual's discrimination as well as psychological factors that bias his or her judgment. The theory is concerned with the individual's discriminative capacity, or sensitivity that is independent of the judgmental bias or decision criterion the individual may have had when the discrimination was made.

In Table 4.1, an attempt is made to describe the signal detection features of observers who have noticed and discover white-collar crime. Signal intensity, signal alertness, pattern recognition, and personal experience are derived from signal detection theory as characteristics of detection ability.

Pattern recognition is a matter of sense making and contextualization. Contextualization captures the ongoing process of understanding and explaining relationships between information elements.

We argue that signal intensity regarding tips to journalists normally is high, as whistleblowers tend to be upset and want to get attention. Furthermore, we suggest that signal alertness is high among journalists, as they are dependent on tips in their daily work of covering news stories. The issue of pattern recognition is not obvious for journalists, since they often present fragments on a publishing basis, rather than a complete and consistent story of events. Personal experience will vary among journalists who may or may not have been writing about white-collar crime before, depending on the extent of specialization among journalists in the newspaper.

The idea of Table 10.4 is to apply four characteristics of signal detection theory to the detection of white-collar crime. At this stage, the items and values represent exploratory research that needs further study to be trustworthy. Both selection of characteristics as well as judgment on these characteristics for each crime detection source need multiple raters to enable inter-rater reliability to be computed.

However, this is an interesting personal experiment. For example, the police in Norway are a passive recipient of signals. Norwegian police are not under cover in financial markets and have no informants in business corporations. Therefore, police opportunity to receive signals is very limited.

Based on a sample of 369 convicted white-collar criminals in Norway from 2009 to 2015, where 97 offenders were detected by journalists and 272 were detected by others, we found some interesting differences between the two groups (see Table 10.2 earlier). In statistical terms, significant differences can be found in terms of the sum of money involved in crime, and personal finances as registered by the internal revenue service.

Table 10.4 Characteristics of stimulus in detection of white-collar crime

Rank	Crime detection source	Signal intensity	Signal alertness	Pattern recognition	Personal experience	Total score
1	Journalists	High	High	Low	Medium	9
2	Crime victims	High	Low	Medium	Low	7
3	Bankruptcy attorneys	Low	Low	Medium	Medium	6
4	Internal auditors	Low	Medium	Medium	Medium	7
5	Tax authority clerks	Low	Medium	Low	Medium	6
6	Bank employees	Low	Medium	Low	Low	5
7	External auditors	Low	Medium	Medium	Low	6
8	Police officers	Low	Medium	High	Low	7
9	Stock exchange clerks	Low	Low	Medium	Low	5
10	Other sources	–	–	–	–	–

One reason for the high signal alertness among journalists is their complete dependence on external tips to produce news stories. Journalists always need sources to which they have no access unless the sources cooperate with the media. By being polite and receptive, journalists increase the likelihood that whistleblowers and others will contact the media when they learn of potential misconduct and crime.

There seems to be a lot to learn from investigative media and their journalists. Rather than formal procedures often applied on a routine basis by auditors and internal controllers, information sources in terms of those in networks seem to be a more fruitful approach to the detection of white-collar crime.

Szalma and Hancock (2013: 1741) argue that signal detection theory has provided perhaps the most useful analytical tool for evaluating human performance in detection domains:

> The theory permits the independent evaluation of perceptual sensitivity and response bias. Perceptual sensitivity depends upon the perceptual ability of the observer to detect a signal or target or to discriminate signal from no signal events. Response bias represents the operator's decision criterion as to their propensity to say yes or no given the evidence to be evaluated.

If there is a signal and a response, then the observer makes a hit. If there is no signal, but nevertheless a response, then the observer creates a false alarm. If there is a signal, but there is no response, then the observer makes a miss. If there is no signal and no response, then the observer creates a correct rejection. However, this absolute division may not always represent an accurate depiction of the true state of the world (Szalma and Hancock 2013: 1741):

> In many instances, events are sufficiently complex and/or perceptually ambiguous that they possess ongoing properties of both signal and non-signal to varying degrees. It is important to note that this complexity does not result from low versus high signal strength (i.e., changes in the magnitude of the evidence variable) but rather a change in the nature of the evidence variable itself. That is, until absolute categorical identification has occurred (often after the fact), the signal itself may retain various non-signal properties and vice versa. Indeed, it is such categorical (and often multidimensional) blending that induces at least some of the inherent stimulus-based uncertainty in decision-making in the first place. This circumstance is especially true of real-world operational settings.

In our context of crime detection, there can be a signal of crime or no signal of crime from an event or a stimulus. However, an event or a stimulus can send both a signal of crime and at the same time a signal of no crime. The signal of crime can be stronger or weaker than the no signal. A possible range for an event or a stimulus dimension might be from zero (100% membership of the no signal category) to one (100% membership of the signal category). These endpoints correspond to the dichotomous signal detection theory. Values between zero and one reflect different degrees of membership in the two categories (Szalma and Hancock 2013: 1742):

> A signal value of .5 represents maximal uncertainty in the category membership status of the stimulus itself because a stimulus with a signal value of .5 has properties of both a non-signal and a signal to an equal degree. Implicit in this model is the assumption that signal uncertainty exists not only within the observer but also in the state-of-the-world itself.

Szalma and Hancock (2013) suggest a fuzzy signal detection theory where stimuli do not fall into discrete, mutually exclusive categories. The fuzzy theory allows events to simultaneously be in more than one category (e.g., both signal and non-signal). In our context of crime detection, stimuli may be perceived in terms of signal probability, where a stimulus can be perceived as probably a signal or probably not a signal.

Crime signal detection is not only an individual issue. Team cognition may influence individual signal detection. Team cognition, defined as the cognitive activity that occurs within a team, is one of the key factors enhancing team performance. When team members hold convergent perspectives and knowledge, developing team cognition can be a success. On the other hand, breakdown of team cognition concerning the situation can lead to failures in coordination and cause lack of signal detection.

Crime signal detection ability and skill link to general investigative professionalism that includes the ability to collect and evaluate information, the ability to make an analysis, the ability to have specific knowledge of the field, the skill of being careful and meticulous, the skill of looking at different angels, the ability to be intelligent and use intelligence, and the ability to perform a professional inquiry.

Bond (2008) studied signal detection in deception. They carried out experiments where experts had to discriminate between offenders and non-offenders. They specifically investigated law enforcement practitioners' expertise in detecting deception in paroled felons. In signal detection analysis, experts showed high discrimination and did not evidence biased responding. The experts exploited non-verbal cues to make fast, accurate decisions.

Lack of Crime Signal Detection

Signal detection theory provides a general framework to describe and study decisions that are made in uncertain and ambiguous situations. Without sufficient information in a noisy environment with many impressions not linked to any particular signal, it is indeed difficult to detect a crime signal.

External auditors receive an average score of six in Table 3.1. The signal intensity is often low, auditors' signal alertness is medium, auditors' pattern recognition is medium, and their personal experience is often low.

Hestnes (2017) studied a case in Norway to discuss the lack of crime signal detection by auditors. The case concerns a company where the CFO was convicted and sent to prison for embezzlement. The auditor never detected the embezzlement, although it went on for several years. The case is used in Hestnes' book twice, since the detection of embezzlement by others caused an internal investigation. The CFO is discussed as an entrepreneur in white-collar crime, and he is described also in the crime investigation at Hadeland Broadband Network.

Hestnes (2017) conducted semi-structured interviews with a number of people who knew the embezzlement case very well. The results of the case study correspond to crime signal detection theory on the grounds that embezzlement in the company was not detected. Lack of detection was due to the auditor's low score on the four factors in the theory. The findings indicate that the auditor's lack of signal alertness in particular combined with low signal intensity from the audit context was the main reason why the crime was not revealed. Low signal intensity seems to be a result of a financial manager's independent position and the company's ineffective control environment.

In order to be able to detect fraud, the revealing party must be able both physically and mentally to detect signals of misconduct. Signal alertness is a unique readiness to recognize misconduct opportunities where they exist. Auditors are obliged to be aware that fraud may occur, while audit assignments may not necessarily be specifically aimed at detecting fraud unless there are incidents creating suspicion during the auditing process. International auditing standards place great emphasis on the auditor being able to show professional skepticism. The auditing standard ISA 200, paragraph A20, states that professional skepticism increases the auditor's vigilance to identify contradictory audit evidence, "unreliable documentation and responses to requests", "circumstances that may indicate fraud", and other circumstances that require "audit procedures beyond those required of the ISAs". Lack of professional skepticism makes the auditor less aware of abnormal conditions and can cause the auditor to "make false assumptions" for the selection of "audit procedures and evaluation of their results".

However, the auditor will normally not be the one to receive direct signals concerning the occurrence of fraud. White-collar offenders strive to conceal their actions, and most fraud will be well hidden and difficult to detect. In the CFO case, the problem is even greater for the auditor, since the CFO is in a role that typically provides the auditor with access to accounting figures. Therefore, the auditor's signal alertness will be a result of how much the auditor's focus is on risk assessment actions associated with the audit, and also what risk signals the auditor receives through documentation from and communication with a company's board, management, and employees.

A distinction in auditing has been made between alert and non-alert individuals. An alert individual is defined as a person who is able to perceive that characteristics in the environment change, and that the appropriate action must be adapted to the actual situation. A non-alert person fails to perceive or ignores altered signals from the environment. That way, a non-alert person's actions will no longer be appropriate and effective as they used to be.

It seems that an audit becomes less effective in situations where the same auditor has been responsible for several consecutive years of audit. Alertness deteriorates as no deviance occurs. By using the theory of entrepreneurial alertness on the role of the auditor in such situations, it may be argued that the auditor, over time, will gradually lean towards becoming a non-alert individual. This conception is supported by previous research that determines why the auditor does not detect fraud.

A distinction can also be made between formal audit and substance audit. Formalities and systems are checked in a formal audit, while transactions and actors are checked in a substance audit. An argument that the auditor is trained to conduct formal audit is that the auditor's main objective is to obtain confirmation that the accounts are properly prepared. The auditor develops an opinion concerning the accuracy of accounts, and thus, in lesser detail, looks for errors. This approach may limit and even exclude substance control. The auditor may fall in to the confirmation trap by simply checking that the accounts are in accordance with laws and regulations. The auditor neglects to carry out sufficiently detailed tests for factors that may cause red flags to appear. One reason for this neglect might be an auditor's limited cognitive capacity, which is dependent on intelligence and creativity to detect new signals.

References

Albrecht, C. C., Albrecht, W. S., & Dunn, J. G. (2001). Can Auditors Detect Fraud: A Review of the Research Evidence. *Journal of Forensic Accounting, II*, 1–12.

Beasley, M. S. (2003). SAS No. 99: A New Look at Auditor Detection of Fraud. *Journal of Forensic Accounting, IV*, 1–20.

Bond, G. D. (2008). Deception Detection Expertise. *Law and Human Behavior, 32*, 339–351.

Campbell, F. (1997). Journalistic Construction of News: Information Gathering. *New Library World, 98*(2), 60–64.

Drage, K., & Olstad, T. (2008). *Ekstern revisor og økonomisk kriminalitet – En analyse av revisors ansvar og brukernes forventninger* [External Auditor and Financial Crime – An Analysis of Auditor Responsibility and User Expectations]. Oslo: BI Norwegian School of Management.

Farrell, B. R., & Healy, P. (2000). White Collar Crime: A Profile of the Perpetrator and an Evaluation of the Responsibilities for Its Prevention and Detection. *Journal of Forensic Accounting, I*, 17–34.

Gomulya, D., & Mishina, Y. (2017). Signaler Credibility, Signal Susceptibility, and Relative Reliance on Signals: How Stakeholders Change Their Evaluative Processes After Violation of Expectations and Rehabilitative Efforts. *Academy of Management Journal, 60*(2), 554–583.

Hestnes, M. (2017). *Hvorfor avdekket ikke revisor underslaget i Hadeland og Ringerike Bredbånd?* [Why Did the Auditor Not Detect Embezzlement at Hadeland and Ringerike Broadband?] (Master of Science Thesis). Oslo: BI Norwegian Business School.

Huff, M. J., & Bodner, G. E. (2013). When Does Memory Monitoring Succeed Versus Fail? Comparing Item-Specific and Relational Encoding in the DRM Paradigm. *Journal of Experimental Psychology: Learning, Memory, and Cognition, 39*(4), 1246–1256.

Iver, N., & Samociuk, M. (2006). *Fraud and Corruption: Prevention and Detection*. Farnham: Gower Publishing.

Jones, P. (2004). *Fraud and Corruption in Public Services: A Guide to Risk and Prevention*. Aldershot: Gower Publishing.

Liu, G., et al. (2014). Lax Decision Criteria Lead to Negativity Bias: Evidence from the Emotional Stroop Task. *Psychological Reports, 114*(3), 896–912. http://journals.sagepub.com/doi/10.2466/28.04.PR0.114k29w0

Moyes, G. D., & Baker, C. R. (2003). Auditor's Beliefs About the Fraud Detection Effectiveness of Standard Audit Procedures. *Journal of Forensic Accounting, IV*, 199–216.

Olsen, A. B. (2007). *Økonomisk kriminalitet: avdekking, gransking og forebygging* [Financial Crime: Detection, Investigation and Prevention]. Oslo: Universitetsforlaget.

Øvrebø, T. (2004). *Nyhetsproduksjon – kjønn og makt. En studie av endring i Dagsavisen 2000–2003* [News Production – Sex and Power. A Study of Change in Dagsavisen (Norwegian Daily Newspaper) 2000–2003]. Hovedoppgave i Medievitenskap (Master Thesis in Media Science). Universitetet i Oslo (University of Oslo).

Proba. (2011). *Misbruk av sykepengeordningen i folketrygden* [Abuse of Sick Pay Scheme in National Insurance]. Oslo: Proba samfunnsanalyse.

Proba. (2013). *Trygdesvindel i Norge: En kartlegging av fem stønadsordninger* [Social Security Fraud in Norway: A Survey of Five Support Areas]. Oslo: Proba samfunnsanalyse.

Rendal, S., & Westerby, T. (2010). *Hvilke forventninger har revisor i forhold til brukere av finansiell informasjon når det gjelder revisors plikter til forebygging og avdekking av mislighter?* [What Expectations Does the Auditor Have in Relation to Users av Financial Information Concerning Auditor Responsibility for Prevention and Detection of Misconduct?]. [S. Rendal], Oslo.

Silverstone, H., & Sheetz, M. (2003). *Forensic Accounting and Fraud Investigation for Non-experts*. Hoboken: Wiley.

Szalma, J. L., & Hancock, P. A. (2013). A Signal Improvement to Signal Detection Analysis: Fuzzy SDT on the ROCs. *Journal of Experimental Psychology: Human Perception and Performance, 39*(6), 1741–1762.

Terum, L. I., Torsvik, G., & Øverbye, E. (2017). Discrimination Against Ethnic Minorities in Activation Programme? Evidence from a Vignette Experiment. *Journal of Social Policy*, 1–18. https://doi.org/10.1017/S00472794 17000113. Published online: 13 March 2017.

Open Access This chapter is licensed under the terms of the Creative Commons Attribution 4.0 International License (http://creativecommons.org/licenses/by/4.0/), which permits use, sharing, adaptation, distribution and reproduction in any medium or format, as long as you give appropriate credit to the original author(s) and the source, provide a link to the Creative Commons license and indicate if changes were made.

The images or other third party material in this chapter are included in the chapter's Creative Commons license, unless indicated otherwise in a credit line to the material. If material is not included in the chapter's Creative Commons license and your intended use is not permitted by statutory regulation or exceeds the permitted use, you will need to obtain permission directly from the copyright holder.

Erratum to: White-Collar Crime in the Shadow Economy

Peter Gottschalk, Lars Gunnesdal

ERRATUM TO:

P. Gottschalk, L. Gunnesdal, *White-Collar Crime in the Shadow Economy*,
https://doi.org/10.1007/978-3-319-75292-1

Sponsor Statement was not included in the original publication. This has been included in the copyright page in the revised version.

The updated original online version of this book can be found under
https://doi.org/10.1007/978-3-319-75292-1

© Palgrave Macmillan 2018
P. Gottschalk, L. Gunnesdal, *White-Collar Crime in the Shadow Economy*,
https://doi.org/10.1007/978-3-319-75292-1_11

Conclusion

Abstract This book has contrasted white-collar crime and social security fraud. We have shown the characteristics of the disadvantaged social security scammer versus the gifted white-collar criminal. According to our experts, the damage from white-collar crime is probably at least as large as the damage from social security fraud in an economic sense. In our view, it is not objectively justified in the interests of society for authorities to punch harder and more severely on welfare fraud than on white-collar crime. We believe combating economic crime starts at the top, not at the bottom. According to our experts, one in four felons goes free because of police failure to prioritize financial crime committed by people in the elite of society.

Keywords Class justice • Discrimination • Elite • Imprisonment • NAV • Norway • Police priorities • Punishment • Social security fraud • White-collar crime

In this book, we have contrasted white-collar crime and social security fraud. In Norway, in the fall of 2016, one of the authors said to the media:

> My advice to the police is simple: dismiss social security cases. It is excellent if NAV has efficient control routines and reveals fraud cases. It may have a preventive effect. But reactions to social security fraud are not in proportion to the crime that is executed. I mean that these people should never end up in prison.

One who defrauds NAV for a minor amount has quite a high probability of being caught. That is not the case for a great villain in a Norwegian corporation. The few white-collar criminals who are caught are often acquitted due to lack of evidence, while NAV always has evidence ready and thus get small fraudsters convicted to prison. This is unfair and a form of class justice.

The statement did not go unnoticed. Five identical columns in various Norwegian newspapers the following day underlined how one should "be cautious to signal that social security fraud is not as serious as the majority may think". One editor called it "nonsense" to argue that the police should adjust their priorities in the direction of the big fish: "The signal effect is substantial. Social security fraudsters should know that NAV is not asleep."

We think this book has shown that white-collar crime is probably a greater social problem than social security fraud in society. In our view, it is neither thorough nor objectively justified in the interests of society if it is the case that the authorities punch harder and more spectacularly at on welfare fraud than on white-collar crime.

We would say that such discrimination expresses and segments the pre-democratic approach to crime where the criminals, seen from the social elite standpoint, are always "someone else", i.e. "those down there"—the poor, the unemployed, the marginalized, the foreign, or those the elite in Britain used to call "the dangerous classes".

The combination of care for the poor and imprisonment was invented by the emerging modern state to deal with the growing flood of unemployed, beggars, and other poor people. Punishment was not just about reducing crime insecurity, but about dealing with the hierarchical society of social insecurity.

White-collar crime is not committed by the poor, the defeated, or the unemployed, but by people in positions of power, often high up the social ladder. There is a danger that white-collar crime is not perceived as real crime, because it does not include violence and is carried out by better-off citizens.

Imprisonment is not only removal of freedom, but also a stigma. The penalty is a state-sanctioned deprivation of individual glory. When a member of the elite breaks the law, it can result in a problematic situation for others within the elite. An "elite" human's crime can threaten the elite's chastity in a manner that offences committed by "sub-humans" do not.

While a white-collar criminal's actions can threaten the legitimacy of the existing hierarchy of high and low positions, between the honest and virtuous ones on the one side and the dishonest and dishonorable on the other, a social security fraudster's actions will confirm and reinforce the same hierarchy. Could this be a reason why representatives of the social elite are more likely to strike hard and visibly more forcefully on welfare fraud, while they rarely hold up white-collar criminals as a social problem, despite the fact that white-collar crime probably costs us much more than social security fraud? Is this the reason why petty thieves, drug addicts, and NAV fraudsters dominate everyday life in Norwegian courtrooms, since they are considered major problems in society, while the corruption defendant from the executive suite is an unfortunate single case and moreover did not mean it anyway?

This book has presented two illustrative examples of how a social security fraudster and a white-collar criminal respectively are treated in the courts. We know of more major cases that NAV has highlighted, characterized by systematic fraud in networks. Such cases do naturally have a different severity than the case with the fortune teller. But, at the same time, we know of financial crime cases that were far more serious than the CEO case that we have presented.

So, what should the police prioritize in their investigations—social security fraud or white-collar crime? It is probably pretty obvious by now what we think about this matter. We have shown that the damage from white-collar crime is at least as major as the damage from social security fraud in an economic sense. We have shown the characteristics of the disadvantaged social security scammer versus the gifted white-collar criminal. We believe combating economic crime starts at the top, not at the bottom. Why on earth should the bottom people follow laws and regulations when on a daily basis they see in the media that the elite gets away with all kinds of misconduct.

With 1200 to 1500 individuals reported for social security fraud every year, substantial police and prosecution resources are taken up with minor criminal cases. The question is whether this is an appropriate use of resources, or whether the police should instead dismiss the majority of cases and only legally pursue the largest and most organized fraudsters. Although white-collar cases can be far more costly than social security matters for law enforcement, it is important to have a form of criminal justice. There is supposed to be equality before the law.

CONCLUSION

Most white-collar crime cases never end up in police hands. Our experts believe that 59 percent of all white-collar criminals are never detected. The detected 41 percent are not all followed up: 19 percent are not investigated, 8 percent are not prosecuted, 5 percent are not convicted, while only 9 percent are convicted. When 8 percent are not prosecuted, it is often because the police failed to provide adequate evidence. Thus, according to our experts, $19 + 8 = 27$ percent—or one in four felons—go free because of police failure to prioritize financial crime committed by the elite in society.

REFERENCES

ACFE. (2008). *2008 Report to the Nation – On Occupational Fraud & Abuse.* Austin: Association of Certified Fraud Examiners.
ACFE. (2014). *Report to the Nations on Occupational Fraud and Abuse, 2014 Global Fraud Study.* Austin: Association of Certified Fraud Examiners.
ACFE. (2016). *CFE Code of Professional Standard.* Association of Certified Fraud Examiners. www.acfe.com/standards/
Adler, P. S., & Kwon, S. W. (2002). Social Capital. Prospects for a New Concept. *Academy of Management Review, 27*(1), 17–40.
Agder. (2015, September 30). Case LA-2015-195071, *Agder lagmannsrett* [Agder Court of Appeals].
Agnew, R. (2005). *Pressured into Crime. An Overview of General Strain Theory.* Oxford: Oxford University Press.
Agnew, R. (2012). Reflection on "A Revised Strain Theory of Delinquency". *Social Forces, 91*(1), 33–38.
Agnew, R. (2014). Social Concern and Crime: Moving Beyond the Assumption of Simple Self-Interest. *Criminology, 52*(1), 1–32.
Aguilera, R. V., & Vadera, A. K. (2008). The Dark Side of Authority: Antecedents, Mechanisms, and Outcomes of Organizational Corruption. *Journal of Business Ethics, 77,* 431–449.
Ahrne, G., & Brunsson, N. (2011). Organization Outside Organizations: The Significance of Partial Organization. *Organization, 18*(1), 83–104.
Albrecht, C. C., Albrecht, W. S., & Dunn, J. G. (2001). Can Auditors Detect Fraud: A Review of the Research Evidence. *Journal of Forensic Accounting, II,* 1–12.

Alstadsæter, A., Johannesen, N., & Zucman, G. (2017). *Tax Evasion and Inequality* (Working Paper). Paper and Data Appendix available at: http://gabriel-zucman.eu

Altindag, D. T. (2012). Crime and Unemployment: Evidence from Europe. *International Review of Law and Economics, 32*, 145–157.

Anders, S. B. (2006, August). Website of the Month: Association of Certified Fraud Examiners. *The CPA Journal*, p. 71.

Andersen, J. J., Johannesen, N., Lassen, D. D., & Paltseva, E. (2017). Petro Rents, Political Institutions, and Hidden Wealth: Evidence from Offshore Bank Accounts. Journal of the European Economic Association, Volume 15, Issue 4, 1 August 2017, Pages 818–860. https://academic.oup.com/jeea/article-abstract/15/4/818/2965613

Ashforth, B. E., Gioia, D. A., Robinson, S. L., & Trevino, L. K. (2008). Re-reviewing Organizational Corruption. *Academy of Management Review, 33*(3), 670–684.

Ashkanasy, N. M. (2016). Why We Need Theory in the Organization Sciences. *Journal of Organizational Behavior, 37*(8), 1126–1131.

Baird, J. E., & Zelin, R. C. (2009, January). An Examination of the Impact of Obedience Pressure on Perceptions of Fraudulent Acts and the Likelihood of Committing Occupational Fraud. *Journal of Forensic Studies in Accounting & Business, 1*(1), 1–14.

Beasley, M. S. (2003). SAS No. 99: A New Look at Auditor Detection of Fraud. *Journal of Forensic Accounting, IV*, 1–20.

Bendahan, S., Zehnder, C., Pralong, F. P., & Antonakis, J. (2015). Leader Corruption Depends on Power and Testosterone. *The Leadership Quarterly, 26*, 101–122.

Benson, M. L., & Simpson, S. S. (2015). *Understanding White-Collar Crime: An Opportunity Perspective*. New York: Routledge.

Berry, L. L., Seiders, K., & Grewal, D. (2002). Understanding Service Convenience. *Journal of Marketing, 66*, 1–17.

Blickle, G., Schlegel, A., Fassbender, P., & Klein, U. (2006). Some Personality Correlates of Business White-Collar Crime. *Applied Psychology: An International Review, 55*(2), 220–233.

Bogen, T. (2008). *Hvor var du, historien om mitt liv* [Where Were You, the Story of My Life]. Oslo: Schibsted Publishing.

Bond, G. D. (2008). Deception Detection Expertise. *Law and Human Behavior, 32*, 339–351.

Bookman, Z. (2008). Convergences and Omissions in Reporting Corporate and White Collar Crime. *DePaul Business & Commercial Law Journal, 6*, 347–392.

Bradshaw, E. A. (2015). "Obviously, We're All Oil Industry": The Criminogenic Structure of the Offshore Oil Industry. *Theoretical Criminology, 19*(3), 376–395.

Breusch, T. (2005). *Estimating the Underground Economy Using MIMIC Models.* Paper provided by EconWPA in its series Econometrics with number 0507003. http://econwpa.repec.org/eps/em/papers/0507/0507003.pdf

Brody, R. G., & Perri, F. S. (2016). Fraud Detection Suicide: The Dark Side of White-Collar Crime. *Journal of Financial Crime, 23*(4), 786–797.

Brooks, G., & Button, M. (2011). The Police and Fraud Investigation and the Case for a Nationalized Solution in the United Kingdom. *The Police Journal, 84*, 305–319.

Bucy, P. H., Formby, E. P., Raspanti, M. S., & Rooney, K. E. (2008). Why Do They Do It?: The Motives, Mores, and Character of White Collar Criminals. *St. John's Law Review, 82*, 401–571.

Campbell, F. (1997). Journalistic Construction of News: Information Gathering. *New Library World, 98*(2), 60–64.

Carpenter, M. A., & Wade, J. B. (2002). Microlevel Opportunity Structures as Determinants of Non-CEO Executive Pay. *Academy of Management Journal, 45*(6), 1085–1103.

Cebula, R. J. (2012). Revisiting Property Crime and Economic Conditions: An Exploratory Study to Identify Predictive Indicators Beyond Unemployment Rates – Comment. *The Social Science Journal, 49*, 314–316.

Ceccato, V., & Benson, M. L. (2016). Tax Evasion in Sweden 2002–2013: Interpreting Changes in the Rot/Rut Deduction System and Predicting Future Trends. *Crime, Law and Social Change, 66*, 217–232.

CFCS. (2013). *CFCS Certification Examination Study Manual* (4th ed.). Certified Financial Crime Specialist, Association of Certified Financial Crime Specialists, Miami.

CFCS. (2014). *CFCS Certification Examination Study Manual* (4th ed.). Certified Financial Crime Specialist, Association of Certified Financial Crime Specialists, Rivergate Plaza, Miami, 33131.

Chattopadhyay, P., Glick, W. H., & Huber, G. P. (2001). Organizational Actions in Response to Threats and Opportunities. *Academy of Management Journal, 44*(5), 937–955.

Collier, J. E., & Kimes, S. E. (2012). Only If It Is Convenient: Understanding How Convenience Influences Self-Service Technology Evaluation. *Journal of Service Research, 16*(1), 39–51.

Comey, J. B. (2009). Go Directly to Prison: White Collar Sentencing After the Sarbanes-Oxley Act. *Harvard Law Review, 122*, 1728–1749.

Craig, J. M., & Piquero, N. L. (2017). The Effects of Low Self-Control and Desire-for-Control on White-Collar Offending: A Replication. *Deviant Behavior, 37*(11), 1308–1324.

Croall, H. (1989). Who Is the White-Collar Criminal? *The British Journal of Criminology, 29*(2), 157–174.

Dearden, T. E. (2017). An Assessment of Adults' Views on White-Collar Crime. *Journal of Financial Crime, 24*(2), 309–321.

Delegationen. (2008). *Vad koster felen? Omfattning av felaktiga utbetalingar från trygghetssystemen* [What Does the Mistake Cost? Estimation of Wrongful Payments from the Security System]. Stockholm: Delegationen mot felaktiga utbetalningar.

Dhami, M. K. (2007). White-Collar Prisoners' Perceptions of Audience Reaction. *Deviant Behavior, 28*, 57–77.

Dion, M. (2008). Ethical Leadership and Crime Prevention in the Organizational Setting. *Journal of Financial Crime, 15*(3), 308–319.

Dion, M. (2009). Corporate Crime and the Dysfunction of Value Networks. *Journal of Financial Crime, 16*(4), 436–445.

Dodge, M. (2009). *Women and White Collar Crime*. New York: Prentice Hall.

Dollar, D., Fisman, R., & Gatti, R. (2001). Are Women Really the "Fairer" Sex? Corruption and Women in Government. *Journal of Economic Behavior & Organization, 46*(4), 423–429.

Drage, K., & Olstad, T. (2008). *Ekstern revisor og økonomisk kriminalitet – En analyse av revisors ansvar og brukernes forventninger* [External Auditor and Financial Crime – An Analysis of Auditor Responsibility and User Expectations]. Oslo: BI Norwegian School of Management.

Eberl, P., Geiger, D., & Assländer, M. S. (2015). Repairing Trust in an Organization After Integrity Violations. The Ambivalence of Organizational Rule Adjustments. *Organization Studies, 36*(9), 1205–1235.

Eberly, M. B., Holley, E. C., Johnson, M. D., & Mitchell, T. R. (2011). Beyond Internal and External: A Dyadic Theory of Relational Attributions. *Academy of Management Review, 36*(4), 731–753.

Edelbacher, M., Dobovsek, B., & Kratcoski, P. C. (2016). The Relationship of the Informal Economy to Corruption, Fraud, and Organized Crime. In M. Edelbacher, P. C. Kratcoski, & B. Dobovsek (Eds.), *Corruption, Fraud, Organized Crime, and the Shadow Economy*. Boca Raton: CRC Press, Taylor & Francis.

Edelhertz, H. (1970). *The Nature, Impact and Prosecution of White-Collar Crime*. Washington, DC: U.S. Department of Justice.

Eisenhardt, K. M. (1985). Control: Organizational and Economic Approaches. *Management Science, 31*(2), 134–149.

Eisenhardt, K. M. (1989). Building Theories from Case Study Research. *Academy of Management Review, 14*, 532–550.

Elnan, T. S. (2016, April 14, Thursday). –*Kriminelle er ofte mer innovative enn folk flest* [–Criminals Are Often More Innovative than Most People]. Daily Norwegian newspaper *Aftenposten*, part 2, pp. 4–5.

Engdahl, O. (2015). White-Collar Crime and First-Time Adult-Onset Offending: Explorations in the Concept of Negative Life Events as Turning Points. *International Journal of Law, Crime and Justice*, 43(1), 1–16.

Eriksen, T. S. (2010). *Arven etter Ole Christian Bach – et justismord* [The Legacy of Ole Christian Bach – A Miscarriage of Justice]. Oslo: Norgesforlaget Publishing.

Evans, M. (2016). Social Capital and the Shadow Economy. *Journal of Economic Issues*, L(1), 43–58.

Fanelli, A., & Misangyi, V. F. (2006). Bringing Out Charisma: CEO Charisma and External Stakeholders. *Academy of Management Review*, 31(4), 1049–1061.

Farquhar, J. D., & Rowley, J. (2009). Convenience: A Services Perspective. *Marketing Theory*, 9(4), 425–438.

Farrell, B. R., & Healy, P. (2000). White Collar Crime: A Profile of the Perpetrator and an Evaluation of the Responsibilities for Its Prevention and Detection. *Journal of Forensic Accounting*, I, 17–34.

Felson, M., & Boba, R. L. (2010). *Crime and Everyday Life*, Chapter 12: "White-Collar Crime". Thousand Oaks: Sage Publications.

Fosse, G., & Magnusson, G. (2004). *Mayday Mayday! –Kapteinene først i livbåtene!* [Mayday Mayday! –The Captains First in the Lifeboats]. Oslo: Kolofon Publishing.

Galvin, B. M., Lange, D., & Ashforth, B. E. (2015). Narcissistic Organizational Identification: Seeing Oneself as Central to the Organization's Identity. *Academy of Management Review*, 40(2), 163–181.

Gomulya, D., & Mishina, Y. (2017). Signaler Credibility, Signal Susceptibility, and Relative Reliance on Signals: How Stakeholders Change Their Evaluative Processes After Violation of Expectations and Rehabilitative Efforts. *Academy of Management Journal*, 60(2), 554–583.

Gottfredson, M. R., & Hirschi, T. (1990). *A General Theory of Crime*. Stanford: Stanford University Press.

Gottschalk, P. (2015). *Fraud Examiners in White-Collar Crime Investigations*. Boca Raton: CRC Press, Taylor & Francis Publishing.

Gottschalk, P. (2016). *Explaining White-Collar Crime: The Concept of Convenience in Financial Crime Investigations*. London: Palgrave Pivot, Palgrave Macmillan, Springer Publishing.

Gottschalk, P. (2017a). *Understanding White-Collar Crime: A Convenience Perspective*. Boca Raton: CRC Press, Taylor and Francis Publishing.

Gottschalk, P. (2017b). *CEOs and White-Collar Crime: A Convenience Perspective*. London: Palgrave Pivot, Palgrave Macmillan, Springer Publishing.

Gottschalk, P. (2017c). *Organizational Opportunity and Deviant Behavior: Convenience in White-Collar Crime*. Cheltenham: Edward Elgar Publishing.

Gottschalk, P. (2018a). *Investigating White-Collar Crime: Evaluation of Fraud Examinations*. New York: Springer Publishing.

Gottschalk, P. (2018b). *Fraud Investigation: Case Studies of Crime Signal Detection*. London: Routledge Publishing.
Gottschalk, P. (2018c). *Whistleblowing: White-Collar Fraud Signal Detection*. Cambridge: Cambridge Scholars Publishing.
Green, S. P. (2007). *Lying, Cheating, and Stealing*. Oxford: Oxford University Press.
Gulating. (2016, June 27). Case 16-025863AST-GULA/AVD2, *Gulating lagmannsrett* [Gulating Court of Appeals].
Haines, F. (2014). Corporate Fraud as Misplaced Confidence? Exploring Ambiguity in the Accuracy of Accounts and the Materiality of Money. *Theoretical Criminology, 18*(1), 20–37.
Hansen, L. L. (2009). Corporate Financial Crime: Social Diagnosis and Treatment. *Journal of Financial Crime, 16*(1), 28–40.
Heath, J. (2008). Business Ethics and Moral Motivation: A Criminological Perspective. *Journal of Business Ethics, 83*, 595–614.
Hegnar, T. (2017, June 9, Friday). *De superrike og skatt* [The Super-Rich and Tax]. Daily Norwegian financial newspaper *Finansavisen*, p. 2.
Hendriyetty, N., & Grewal, B. S. (2017). Macroeconomics of Money Laundering: Effects and Measurements. *Journal of Financial Crime, 24*(1), 65–81.
Henry, J. (2012). *The Price of Offshore Revisited. New Estimates for "Missing" Global Private Wealth, Income, Inequality, and Lost Taxes*. Tax Justice Network.
Hestnes, M. (2017). *Hvorfor avdekket ikke revisor underslaget i Hadeland og Ringerike Bredbånd?* [Why Did the Auditor Not Detect Embezzlement at Hadeland and Ringerike Broadband?] (Master of Science Thesis). Oslo: BI Norwegian Business School.
Heyman, J., & Sailors, J. (2016). A Respondent-Friendly Method of Ranking Long Lists. *International Journal of Market Research, 58*(5), 693–710.
Hirschi, T., & Gottfredson, M. (1987). Causes of White-Collar Crime. *Criminology, 25*(4), 949–974.
Holtfreter, K. (2015). General Theory, Gender-Specific Theory, and White-Collar Crime. *Journal of Financial Crime, 22*(4), 422–431.
Huff, M. J., & Bodner, G. E. (2013). When Does Memory Monitoring Succeed Versus Fail? Comparing Item-Specific and Relational Encoding in the DRM Paradigm. *Journal of Experimental Psychology: Learning, Memory, and Cognition, 39*(4), 1246–1256.
Huff, R., Desilets, K., & Kane, J. (2010). *The National Public Survey on White Cllar Crime*. Fairmont: National White Collar Crime Center. www.nw3c.org.
Huisman, W., & Erp, J. (2013). Opportunities for Environmental Crime. *British Journal of Criminology, 53*, 1178–1200.
Imamoglu, H. (2016). Re-estimation of the Size of Underground Economy in European Countries: MIMIC Approach. *International Journal of Economic Perspectives, 10*(1), 171–193.

Iver, N., & Samociuk, M. (2006). *Fraud and Corruption: Prevention and Detection*. Farnham: Gower Publishing.

Jacobsen, S. K., & Coll, I. A. E. (2017, June 10, Saturday). *Galskap å legge ned Økokrim* [Madness to Close Down Økokrim (Norwegian National Authority for Investigation and Prosecution of Economic and Environmental Crime)]. Daily Norwegian Business Newspaper *Dagens Næringsliv*, p. 28.

Jones, S. (2014). Internal Report Details GM Ignition Coverup. *World Socialist Web Site*. Published June 14. http://www.wsws.org/en/articles/2014/06/14/genm-j14.html. Downloaded December 2, 2014.

Jones, P. (2004). *Fraud and Corruption in Public Services: A Guide to Risk and Prevention*. Aldershot: Gower Publishing. https://books.google.no/books?id=Pz9IWxPrZ8C&dq=A+persistent+debate+has+dogged+relationships+between+auditors+and+managers.&hl=no&source=gbs_navlinks_s

Jonnergård, K., Stafsudd, A., & Elg, U. (2010). Performance Evaluations as Gender Barriers in Professional Organizations: A Study of Auditing Firms. *Gender, Work and Organization, 17*(6), 721–747.

Kang, E., & Thosuwanchot, N. (2017). An Application of Durkheim's Four Categories of Suicide to Organizational Crimes. *Deviant Behavior, 38*(5), 493–513.

Kaspersen, L. (2017). Ber sjefen gripe inn mot juks med sykemeldinger. *Dagens Næringsliv*, mandag 12. januar, side 22–23.

Kempa, M. (2010). Combating White-Collar Crime in Canada: Serving Victim Needs and Market Integrity. *Journal of Financial Crime, 17*(2), 251–264.

Kerik, B. B. (2005). *From Jailer to Jailed – My Journey from Correction and Police Commissioner to Inmate #84888-054*. New York: Threshold Editions.

Kostelnik, J. (2012). Sentencing White-Collar Criminals: When Is Shaming Viable? *Global Crime, 13*(3), 141–159.

Kouchaki, M., & Desai, S. D. (2015). Anxious, Threatened, and Also Unethical: How Anxiety Makes Individuals Feel Threatened and Commit Unethical Acts. *Journal of Applied Psychology, 100*(2), 360–375.

Kynn, M. (2008). The 'Heuristics and Biases' Bias in Expert Elicitation. *Journal of the Royal Statistical Society, 171*, 239–264.

Lancaster, K. (2017). Confidentiality, Anonymity and Power Relations in Elite Interviewing: Conducting Quality Policy Research in a Politicized Domain. *International Journal of Social Research Methodology, 20*(1), 93–103.

Langton, L., & Piquero, N. L. (2007). Can General Strain Theory Explain White-Collar Crime? A Preliminary Investigation of the Relationship Between Strain and Select White-Collar Offenses. *Journal of Criminal Justice, 35*, 1–15.

Leasure, P., & Zhang, G. (2017). "That's How They Taught Us to Do It": Learned Deviance and Inadequate Deterrents in Retail Banking. *Deviant Behavior*. Published online 28 February. https://doi.org/10.1080/01639625.2017.1286179.

Lee, F., & Robinson, R. J. (2000). An Attributional Analysis of Social Accounts: Implications of Playing the Blame Game. *Journal of Applied Social Psychology, 30*(9), 1853–1879.

Lensvelt-Mulders, G. J. L. M., Heijden, P. G. M., & Laudy, O. (2006). A Validation of a Computer-Assisted Randomized Response Survey to Estimate the Prevalence of Fraud in Social Security. *Journal of the Royal Statistical Society, 169*, 305–318.

Leonard, W. N., & Weber, M. G. (1970). Automakers and Dealers: A Study of Criminogenic Market Forces. *Law and Society Review, 4*(3), 407–424.

Levi, M. (2002). Suite Justice or Sweet Charity? Some Explorations of Shaming and Incapacitating Business Fraudsters. *Punishment & Society, 4*(2), 147–163.

Liang, L. H., Lian, H., Brown, D. J., Ferris, D. L., Hanig, S., & Keepoing, L. M. (2016). Why Are Abusive Supervisors Abusive? A Dual-System Self-Control Model. *Academy of Management Journal, 59*(4), 1385–1406.

Liu, G., et al. (2014). Lax Decision Criteria Lead to Negativity Bias: Evidence from the Emotional Stroop Task. *Psychological Reports, 114*(3), 896–912. http://journals.sagepub.com/doi/10.2466/28.04.PR0.114k29w0

Liu, G., & Ren, H. (2017). Ethical Team Leadership and Trainee Auditors' Likelihood of Reporting Client's Irregularities. *Journal of Financial Crime, 24*(1), 157–175.

Logan, M. W (2015). *Coping with Imprisonment: Testing the Special Sensitivity Hypothesis for White-Collar Offenders*. A dissertation to the Graduate School of the University of Cincinnati in partial fulfilment of the requirements for the degree of Doctor of Philosophy in the Department of Criminal Justice, Cincinnati.

Lord, N. (2016). Establishing Enforcement Legitimacy in the Pursuit of Rule-Breaking 'Global Elites': The Case of Transnational Corporate Bribery. *Theoretical Criminology, 20*(3), 376–399.

Mai, H. T. X., & Olsen, S. O. (2016). Consumer Participation in Self-Production: The Role of Control Mechanisms, Convenience Orientation, and Moral Obligation. *Journal of Marketing Theory and Practice, 24*(2), 209–223.

Mann, K., Wheeler, K., & Sarat, A. (1979). Sentencing the White Collar Defender. *American Criminal Law Review, 17*, 479–500.

McGurrin, D., Jarrell, M., Jahn, A., & Cochrane, B. (2013). White Collar Crime Representation in the Criminological Literature Revisited, 2001–2010. *Western Criminology Review, 14*(2), 3–19.

McKay, R., Stevens, C., & Fratzi, J. (2010). A 12-Step Process of White-Collar Crime. *International Journal of Business Governance and Ethics, 5*(1), 14–25.

McKeever, G. (2012). Social Citizenship and Social Security Fraud in the UK and Australia. *Social Policy & Administration, 46*(4), 465–482.

McKenndal, M. A., & Wagner, J. A. (1997). Motive, Opportunity, Choice, and Corporate Illegality. *Organization Science, 8*, 624–647.

Mertens, W., Recker, J., Kohlborn, T., & Kummer, T. F. (2016). A Framework for the Study of Positive Deviance in Organizations. *Deviant Behavior, 37*(11), 1288–1307.

Meyer, M. A., & Booker, J. M. (2001). *Eliciting and Analyzing Expert Judgment: A Practical Guide, SIAM Books, ASA-SIAM Series on Statistics and Applied Probability*. Philadelphia: Society for Industrial and Applied Mathematics (SIAM).

Michel, P. (2008). Financial Crimes: The Constant Challenge of Seeking Effective Prevention Solutions. *Journal of Financial Crime, 15*(4), 383–397.

Montella, E. C. (2016). *Full Circle: A Memoir of Leaning in Too Far and the Journey Back*. Sanibel: Triple M Press.

Moyes, G. D., & Baker, C. R. (2003). Auditor's Beliefs About the Fraud Detection Effectiveness of Standard Audit Procedures. *Journal of Forensic Accounting, IV*, 199–216.

Naylor, R. T. (2003). Towards a General Theory of Profit-Driven Crimes. *British Journal of Criminology, 43*, 81–101.

Nelken, D. (2012). White-Collar and Corporate Crime. In M. Maguire, R. Morgan, & R. Reiner (Eds.), *The Oxford Handbook of Criminology*. Oxford: Oxford University Press.

O'Connor, T. R. (2005). Police Deviance and Ethics. I: *Part of Web Cited, MegaLinks in Criminal Justice*. http://faculty.ncwc.edu/toconnor/205/205lect11.htm. Lasted ned 19. februar 2009.

O'Fallon, M., & Butterfield, K. D. (2005). A Review of the Empirical Ethical Decision-Making Literature: 1996–2003. *Journal of Business Ethics, 59*(4), 375–413.

Olsen, A. B. (2007). *Økonomisk kriminalitet: avdekking, gransking og forebygging* [Financial Crime: Detection, Investigation and Prevention]. Oslo: Universitetsforlaget.

Onna, J. H. R., Geest, V. R., Huisman, W., & Denkers, J. M. (2014). Criminal Trajectories of White-Collar Offenders. *Journal of Research in Crime and Delinquency, 51*, 759–784.

Osterburg, J. W., & Ward, R. H. (2014). *Criminal Investigation: A Method for Reconstructing the Past* (7th ed.). Waltham: Anderson Publishing.

Ouimet, G. (2009). Psychology of White-Collar Criminal: In Search of Personality. *Psychologie Du Travail Et Des Organisations, 15*(3), 297–320.

Ouimet, G. (2010). Dynamics of Narcissistic Leadership in Organizations. *Journal of Managerial Psychology, 25*(7), 713–726.

Øvrebø, T. (2004). *Nyhetsproduksjon – kjønn og makt. En studie av endring i Dagsavisen 2000–2003* [News Production – Sex and Power. A Study of Change in Dagsavisen (Norwegian Daily Newspaper) 2000–2003]. Hovedoppgave i

Medievitenskap (Master Thesis in Media Science). Universitetet i Oslo (University of Oslo).

Pangrazio, L. (2017). Exploring Provocation as a Research Method in the Social Sciences. *International Journal of Social Research Methodology*. Published online https://doi.org/10.1080/13645579.2016.1161346.

Perri, F. S. (2011). White-Collar Criminals: The 'Kinder, Gentler' Offender? *Journal of Investigative Psychology and Offender Profiling, 8*(3), 217–241.

Petersen, H. G., Thiessen, U., & Wohlleben, P. (2010). Shadow Economy, Tax Evasion, and Transfer Fraud – Definition, Measurement, and Data Problems. *International Economic Journal, 24*(4), 421–441.

Petrocelli, M., Piquero, A. R., & Smith, M. R. (2003). Conflict Theory and Racial Profiling: An Empirical Analysis of Police Traffic Stop Data. *Journal of Criminal Justice, 31*, 1–11.

Pickett, K. H. S., & Pickett, J. M. (2002). *Financial Crime Investigation and Control*. New York: John Wiley & Sons.

Piquero, N. L. (2012). The Only Thing We Have to Fear Is Fear Itself: Investigating the Relationship Between Fear of Falling and White Collar Crime. *Crime and Delinquency, 58*(3), 362–379.

Piquero, N. L., & Benson, M. L. (2004). White Collar Crime and Criminal Careers: Specifying a Trajectory of Punctuated Situational Offending. *Journal of Contemporary Criminal Justice, 20*, 148–165.

Piquero, N. L., Schoepfer, A., & Langton, L. (2010). Completely Out of Control or the Desire to Be in Complete Control? How Low Self-Control and the Desire for Control Relate to Corporate Offending. *Crime & Delinquency, 56*(4), 627–647.

Pontell, H. N., Black, W. K., & Geis, G. (2014). Too Big to Fail, Too Powerful to Jail? On the Absence of Criminal Prosecutions After the 2008 Financial Meltdown. *Crime, Law and Social Change, 61*(1), 1–13.

Pratt, T. C., & Cullen, F. T. (2005). Assessing Macro-Level Predictors and Theories of Crime: A Meta-Analysis. *Crime and Justice, 32*, 373–450.

Proba. (2011). *Misbruk av sykepengeordningen i folketrygden* [Abuse of Sick Pay Scheme in National Insurance]. Oslo: Proba samfunnsanalyse.

Proba. (2013). *Trygdesvindel i Norge: En kartlegging av fem stønadsordninger* [Social Security Fraud in Norway: A Survey of Five Support Areas]. Oslo: Proba samfunnsanalyse.

Punch, M. (2003). Rotten Orchards. «Pestilence», Police Misconduct and System Failure. *Policing and Society, 13*(2), 171–196.

Puranam, P., Alexy, O., & Reitzig, M. (2014). What's «New» About New Forms of Organizing? *Academy of Management Review, 39*(2), 162–180.

Ragatz, L. L., Fremouw, W., & Baker, E. (2012). The Psychological Profile of White-Collar Offenders: Demographics, Criminal Thinking, Psychopathic Traits, and Psychopathology. *Criminal Justice and Behavior, 39*(7), 978–997.

Reed, G. E., & Yeager, P. C. (1996). Organizational Offending and Neoclassical Criminology. Challenging the Reach of a General Theory of Crime. *Criminology, 34*(3), 357–382.

Rendal, S., & Westerby, T. (2010). *Hvilke forventninger har revisor i forhold til brukere av finansiell informasjon når det gjelder revisors plikter til forebygging og avdekking av misligheter?* [What Expectations Does the Auditor Have in Relation to Users av Financial Information Concerning Auditor Responsibility for Prevention and Detection of Misconduct?]. [S. Rendal], Oslo.

Rossmo, D. K., & Routledge, R. (1990). Estimating the Size of Criminal Populations. *Journal of Quantitative Criminology, 6*(3), 293–314.

Samfunnsøkonomisk analyse. (2017). *Analyse av former, omfang og utvikling av arbeidsmarkedskriminalitet* [Analysis of the Forms, Scope and Development of Labor Market Crime]. Oslo: Samfunnsøkonomisk analyse. www.samfunnsokonomisk-analyse.no

Sari, Y. K., Shaari, Z. H., & Amar, A. B. (2017). Measurement Development of Customer Patronage of Petrol Station with Convenience Store. *Global Business and Management Research: An International Journal, 9*(1), 52–62.

Schneider, S. (2006). Privatizing Economic Crime Enforcement: Exploring the Role of Private Sector Investigative Agencies in Combating Money Laundering. *Policing & Society, 16*(3), 285–312.

Schneider, F., & Williams, C. C. (2013). *The Shadow Economy.* London: The Institute of Economic Affairs.

Schneider, F., Buehn, A., & Montenegro, C. E. (2010). *Shadow Economies All over the World: New Estimates for 162 Countries from 1999 to 2007.* The World Bank, Development Research Group, Poverty and Inequality Team. www.gfintegrity.org.

Schoepfer, A., & Piquero, N. L. (2006). Exploring White-Collar Crime and the American Dream: A Partial Test of Institutional Anomie Theory. *Journal of Criminal Justice, 34*, 227–235.

Schwendinger, H., & Schwendinger, J. (2014). Defenders of Order or Guardians of Human Rights? *Social Justice, 40*(1/2), 87–117.

Shapiro, S. P. (1987). The Social Control of Impersonal Trust. *American Journal of Sociology, 93*(3), 623–658.

Shen, W., & Cannella, A. A. (2002). Power Dynamics Within Top Management and Their Impacts on CEO Dismissal Followed by Inside Succession. *Academy of Management Journal, 45*(6), 1195–1206.

Shover, N., Hochsteller, A., & Alalehto, T. (2012). Choosing White-Collar Crime. In F. T. Cullen & P. Wilcox (Eds.), *The Oxford Handbook of Criminological Theory.* Oxford: Oxford University Press.

Siegel, L. J. (2011). *Criminology* (11th ed.). Belmont: Wadsworth Publishing.

Silverstone, H., & Sheetz, M. (2003). *Forensic Accounting and Fraud Investigation for Non-experts*. Hoboken: Wiley.

Siponen, M., & Vance, A. (2010). Neutralization: New Insights into the Problem of Employee Information Security Policy Violations. *MIS Quarterly, 34*(3), 487–502.

Slottje, P., Sluijs, J. P., & Knol, A. B. (2008). *Expert Elicitation: Methodological Suggestions for Its Use in Environmental Health Impact Assessments* (RIVM Letter Report). The Netherlands: National Institute for Public Health and the Environment.

Solem, L. K. (2016, September 25 Friday). *Kan slippe med 10 måneder i fengsel* [Can Get Away with 10 Months in Prison]. Daily Norwegian Business Newspaper *Dagens Næringsliv*, pp. 12–13.

Soltes, E. (2016). *Why They Do It: Inside the Mind of the White-Collar Criminal*. New York: Public Affairs Books.

Stadler, W. A., Benson, M. L., & Cullen, E. T. (2013). Revisiting the Special Sensitivity Hypothesis: The Prison Experience of White-Collar Inmates. *Justice Quarterly, 30*(6), 1090–1114.

Steffensmeier, D., Schwartz, J., & Roche, M. (2013). Gender and Twenty-First-Century Corporate Crime: Female Involvement and the Gender Gap in Enron-Era Corporate Frauds. *American Sociological Review, 5*, 1–12.

Sundström, M., & Radon, A. (2015). Utilizing the Concept of Convenience as a Business Opportunity in Emerging Markets. *Organizations and Markets in Emerging Economies, 6*(2), 7–21.

Supernor, H. (2017). Community Service and White-Collar Offenders: The Characteristics of the Sanction on Factors Determining Its Use Among a Sample of Health-Care Offenders. *Journal of Financial Crime, 24*(1), 148–156.

Sutherland, E. H. (1939). White-Collar Criminality. *American Sociological Review, 5*, 1–12.

Sutherland, E. H. (1949). *White-Collar Crime*. New York: Holt, Rinehart and Winston Publishing.

Sutherland, E. H. (1983). *White Collar Crime – The Uncut Version*. New Haven: Yale University Press.

Sykes, G., & Matza, D. (1957). Techniques of Neutralization: A Theory of Delinquency. *American Sociological Review, 22*(6), 664–670.

Szalma, J. L., & Hancock, P. A. (2013). A Signal Improvement to Signal Detection Analysis: Fuzzy SDT on the ROCs. *Journal of Experimental Psychology: Human Perception and Performance, 39*(6), 1741–1762.

Terum, L. I., Torsvik, G., & Øverbye, E. (2017). Discrimination Against Ethnic Minorities in Activation Programme? Evidence from a Vignette Experiment. *Journal of Social Policy*, 1–18. https://doi.org/10.1017/S0047279417000113. Published online: 13 March 2017.

Valkenhoef, G., & Tervonen, T. (2016). Entropy-Optimal Weight Constraint Elicitation with Additive Multi-attribute Utility Models. *Omega, 64*, 1–12.

Valukas, A. R. (2010, March 11). *In Regard Lehman Brothers Holdings Inc. to United States Bankruptcy Court in Southern District of New York.* Jenner & Block, 239 p. http://www.nysb.uscourts.gov/sites/default/files/opinions/188162_61_opinion.pdf

Valukas, A. R. (2014, May 29). *Report to Board of Directors of General Motors Company Regarding Ignition Switch Recalls.* Law firm Jenner & Block, 325 p. http://www.beasleyallen.com/webfiles/valukas-report-on-gm-redacted.pdf

Weaver, C. N. (1975). Job Preferences of White Collar and Blue Collar Workers. *Academy of Management Journal, 18*(1), 167–175.

Welsh, D. T., Oronez, L. D., Snyder, D. G., & Christian, M. S. (2014). The Slippery Slope: How Small Ethical Transgressions Pave the Way for Larger Future Transgressions. *Journal of Applied Psychology, 100*(1), 114–127.

Yearwood, D. L., & Koinis, G. (2011). Revisiting Property Crime and Economic Conditions: An Exploratory Study to Identify Predictive Indicators Beyond Unemployment Rates. *The Social Science Journal, 48*, 145–158.

Zahra, S. A., Priem, R. L., & Rasheed, A. A. (2007). Understanding the Causes and Effects of Top Management Fraud. *Organizational Dynamics, 36*(2), 122–139.

Zipparo, L. (1999). Factors Which Deter Public Officials from Reporting Corruption. *Crime, Law & Social Change, 30*(3), 273–287.

Zucman, G. (2015). *The Hidden Wealth of Nations. The Scourge of Tax Havens.* The University of Chicago Press. http://gabriel-zucman.eu/hidden-wealth/

Index

A
Auditor detection, 120
Average amount, 28, 29, 39, 64, 115

B
Behavioral willingness, 21–24
Benefits, 6, 7, 16, 17, 19, 74, 75, 79–82, 85, 102, 107, 108, 114, 125
Booker, J. A., 31, 32, 50, 52–54

C
Categories of crime, 28–30, 38, 41–43, 53, 69, 91, 116, 117
Categories of victims, 29, 43, 50, 69
Class justice, 136
Comparison, xii, xiv, 3, 5, 20, 47, 72, 80, 92, 102, 113, 115, 116
Confirmation trap, 65, 132
Convenience theory, 1, 2, 5, 6, 9, 18, 20, 77, 78
Conviction, 10, 12, 30, 38, 39, 41–44, 57–59, 68–70, 76, 82

Conviction rate, 39, 41, 42, 70, 71
Corporate hierarchy, 20
Corruption Detection, 63
Crime detection, xiii, 63, 111–132
Crime detection source, 115, 127
Criminal level, 29
Criminal population size, 61
Criminology, 3–5, 15, 84, 85

D
Database, xii, 28, 68–70
Dealing with outliers, 54–55
Definition, 2, 4, 5, 100, 126
Detection, xiii, 7, 10, 22, 23, 30, 32, 38, 39, 43, 58–65, 70, 72, 78, 81, 89, 94, 96, 99, 113, 115–132
Detection suicide, 23
Deviant behavior, 3, 20, 21, 28
Discrimination, 65, 113, 114, 124, 126, 128–130, 136
Distribution of experts, 50
Diversity of participants, 33

E

Eirik Schea, Trond, 37, 47
Elite, xii, xiii, 2, 3, 7, 9, 10, 16, 18, 20, 27, 32, 78, 86, 101, 102, 113, 136–138
Empirical sample, 28–30
Estimated magnitude, 28, 39, 78, 111, 112
Estimation, ix, xii–xiv, 28–33, 37–47, 49, 50, 53, 54, 57, 59–61, 68–72, 74, 76, 77, 79–83, 89–108
Estimation approaches, 28
Expected utility, 16
Expert elicitation, xii, xiv, 28, 30–32, 37–47, 49–51, 55, 57, 60, 67, 71, 77, 81, 94, 111
Expert judgement inference, 30, 31
External auditor, 32, 51, 52, 59, 115, 121–124, 130

F

Female offenders, 30, 38, 43, 60–63, 65
Financial motive, 18–19, 28, 97
Fraction detected and convicted, 30, 38, 41, 64, 65, 81, 120
Fraud, vii, ix, xii–xiv, 4, 5, 19, 21, 23, 28, 29, 41, 42, 47, 52, 53, 69, 70, 73–86, 91, 94, 95, 97, 100, 101, 103, 106, 112, 113, 116, 117, 120–123, 130, 131, 135–137

G

Gender, 6, 28, 29, 43, 61–65, 70
Gender gap, 61–63, 65
Gender perspectives, 7, 61–65
Gender ratio, 70

H

Hidden wealth, 7, 101–105

I

Imprisonment, 9–11, 61, 75, 76, 79, 136
Internal auditor, 32, 51, 61, 115, 121, 122, 124
Investigation, xii, 2, 37, 47, 52, 58, 63, 65, 70, 72, 85, 121, 122, 125, 130, 137

J

Journalist detection, 115, 117, 120

L

Labor market crime, 50, 93–95

M

Magnitude of crime, ix, xiv, 28, 30, 32, 38, 42–44, 49, 50, 54, 55, 57, 60, 67, 70, 76–78, 91, 94, 106, 111
Manipulation, 29, 41, 42, 53, 60, 69, 91, 117, 119, 125, 126
Media coverage, 10
Median answers, 54
Methodology, 74, 92, 94
Meyer, M. A., 31–33, 50, 52–54
MIMIC approach, 92–98
Money laundering, 90, 98–99

N

NAV, 75, 76, 79–83, 85, 106, 112–114, 135–137
Norway, ix, xii, xiii, 28, 31, 32, 38, 43, 44, 47, 49, 53, 54, 57, 61, 63, 70–72, 74, 77, 78, 82, 83, 86, 92–95, 102, 105, 106, 112–115, 118, 122–125, 127, 130, 135

O

Occupational crime, 8, 95
Offense characeristics, 5–6
Offender characteristics, 6–7
Offender groups, 30, 38, 41, 68
Offshore accounts, 102–106
Organizational opportunity, 20–21, 28

P

Panama Papers, 103, 105, 108
Participation refusal, 32, 50–55
Pink-collar criminals, 63
Police priorities, 83, 137
Probability distribution, 30, 38–40, 45, 60, 68
Prosecution, 5, 37, 47, 58, 72, 84, 85, 137
Psychopathy, 23
Punishment, 6, 136

R

Recruitment of experts, 50, 54, 55
Research design, 32, 50
Response confusion, 32, 50, 53–54
Response rate, 50, 55

S

Screening theory, 126
Self-control, 22, 78
Shadow economy, xiv, 85, 89–93, 97, 100–101
Signal alertness, 125–128, 130, 131
Signal detection theory, 124–130
Size of iceberg, xii, 39
Social conflict theory, xii, 74, 83–86
Social security, 62, 74–79, 82, 85, 91, 94, 101, 106, 108, 112–114, 135, 137
Social security fraud, ix, xii, xiii, 31, 44, 46, 73–86, 94, 106, 112, 113, 135–137

Social status, 2, 3, 5, 6
Sources of detection, 32, 34, 124
Special sensitivity hypothesis, 8–12, 16
Student elicitation, xiv, 68–72
Sutherland, E. H, 1, 3–6, 27, 50, 78

T

Tax evasion, 4, 7, 29, 42, 69, 75, 76, 91, 92, 94–96, 99–102, 104–106, 108, 117
Tax haven, 7, 102–106, 108
Theft, 29, 41, 42, 53, 60, 69, 91, 97, 117
Tip of the iceberg, ix, xi–xii, xiv, 32, 46, 50, 80
Type of crime, 4
Type of offender, 41

U

Uncertainty, ix, xiii, 30, 39, 45, 46, 53, 79, 80, 102, 106, 125, 128, 129
U.S. estimates, 47

V

Variation in responses, 60
Victim groups, 29, 30, 38, 42, 69

W

Whistleblower, 52, 82, 117, 124, 126, 128
White-collar crime, xi, 1–12, 15, 27–28, 38, 49, 57, 68, 73, 89, 111–132, 135

Z

Zucman, Gabriel, 103, 104

The manufacturer's authorised representative in the EU is Springer Nature Customer Service Centre GmbH, Europaplatz 3, 69115 Heidelberg, Germany. If you have any concerns regarding our products, please contact ProductSafety@springernature.com

Printed and bound by CPI Group (UK) Ltd, Croydon, CR0 4YY
23/03/2026
02076447-0015